MILITARY
QUIZ
BOOK

I am not afraid of an army of lions
led by a sheep; I am afraid of
an army of sheep led by a lion.

Alexander the Great

MILITARY QUIZ BOOK

Test Your Knowledge of Warfare Through the Ages

JOHN PIMLOTT

amber
BOOKS

Copyright © 2018 Amber Books Ltd

First published in 1993

Published by Amber Books Ltd
United House
London N7 9DP
United Kingdom
www.amberbooks.co.uk
Appstore: itunes.com/apps/amberbooksltd
Facebook: www.facebook.com/amberbooks
Twitter: @amberbooks

ISBN: 978-1-78274-605-8

Printed in the United States

CONTENTS

Introduction

The *Military Quiz Book* is designed to test, and stretch, the knowledge of military buffs of all ages and persuasions. Some of the questions are easy; some are difficult. Some will stay maddeningly hidden, even though they are on the 'tip of the tongue', while in others the answer will open up new perspectives.

We have set the questions in groups of seven, because that gave the most interesting mix of subjects. Questions have been posed in the following major categories: personalities, battles and campaigns, weapons and equipment, who said what, naval warfare, air warfare (where applicable!), uniforms and decorations, units and formations, civilians, spies and spying, and total trivia. We have further divided up the contents into three broad historical categories.

I should like to thank Steve Badsey, Ashley Brown, Peter Darman and Ian Westwell, fellow military trivia nuts, for their help with specialist areas. We all hope you have as much fun grappling with the questions as we had in setting them.

Dr. John Pimlott

To 1600

Questions 1

a. What role did Odone Doria and Carlo Grimaldi fulfil at Crecy 1346?

b. Who was the Emperor when Rome successfully invaded Britain?

c. Arsuf (1191) was the main triumph of which commander in the Third Crusade?

d. What was a calthrop?

e. What was a petronel?

f. What was lacking in the general who reconquered Italy for the Emperor Justinian during the 6th century?

g. What were aiguillettes?

Questions 2

a. Who commanded the Roman forces that defeated Attila the Hun at Chalons in 451?

b. How many Punic Wars were there?

c. In the 'Combat of the Thirty' (1351), by what underhand method did the French knights achieve victory?

d. Why were Roman javelins constructed with a section of soft metal?

e. What was a fustibal?

f. Who said, 'Success in war depends less on intrepidity than on prudence, to await, to distinguish, and to seize the decisive moment of fortune.'?

g. Which French duke's flag bore the device of a wounded swan?

Questions 3

a. Name the rival commanders at the 1453 siege of Constantinople.

b. Which siege finally ended the resistance of the Gauls to Roman rule?

c. At which battle did Joan of Arc exhort her commanders to attack the English with the following words, 'You have spurs, use them.'?

d. How would Romans have used a 'tortoise'?

e. What does the term janissary mean?

f. From which civilisation was the king who boasted, 'I decimated the enemy host with arrow and spear. All of their bodies I bored through like a sieve ... Like the many waters of a storm I made the contents of their gullets and entrails run down upon the wide earth.'?

g. What was a brigandine?

Answers 1

a. They commanded the French army's ill-fated Genoese crossbowmen.

b. Claudius.

c. Richard I.

d. A sharp, many-pointed device usually of metal, that when scattered could break up enemy cavalry or infantry attacks by piercing hooves or the soles of shoes. (In more modern parlance, a calthrop is a similar device used for stopping wheeled vehicles by piercing the tyres).

e. An early form of handgun.

f. Narses was a eunuch.

g. Armour to protect the shoulder.

Answers 2

a. Aetius.

b. Three.

c. Although the combat was to be on foot, at a vital moment one knight mounted his horse and charged into the English.

d. So they would bend when they penetrated enemy shields, rendering the shields unusable, and also becoming useless themselves.

e. A sling mounted on a staff for throwing large projectiles.

f. Count Belisarius.

g. The Due de Berri.

Answers 3

a. Mohammad II and Constantine XI.

b. Alesia.

c. Patay (1429).

d. To assault a walled city: it was a solid formation where locked shields defended infantry against missiles from the sides and from the top.

e. 'Yeni ceri', literally 'new troops'.

f. Sennacherib, King of Assyria.

g. A jacket lined with iron scales.

Questions 4
a. What disability severely reduced King John of Bohemia's fighting efficiency at Crecy?
b. At what battle did Julius Caesar finally defeat Pompey?
c. What was a heater?
d. The English victory over the Scots at Halidon Hill (1333) saw the advent of which tactical innovation?
e. What ingredients were usually found in a stinkpot?
f. Who said, 'The art of war is, in the last resort, the art of keeping one's freedom of action.'?
g. Whose livery comprised the bear and ragged staff?

Questions 5
a. Which barbarian chieftain sacked Rome in 410 AD?
b. How was Scotland's James II killed in 1460?
c. Where did the Goths destroy the army of the Emperor Valens?
d. What was a bouche?
e. Where in 1187 would you have found God's Own Sling and the Wicked Neighbour?
f. What natural event helped defeat Kublai Khan's 1281 invasion of Japan?
g. What does the Russian term *Streltsi* refer to?

Questions 6
a. Who took command of the famed White Company in 1364?
b. Where, and against whom, did the Maccabean revolt take place?
c. Which battle of 1071 saw the virtual destruction of the Byzantine Empire's regular army?
d. What were the three divisions of a medieval army called?
e. What was a destrier?
f. Although victorious, at which naval battle of 1350 did both Edward III and the Black Prince lose their warships?
g. What was an orta?

Questions 7
a. Who was Lysander?
b. What is considered most significant about the Flemish victory at Courtrai (1302)?
c. What weapon of war did the Italian city of Pavia give to the medieval world?
d. What role did a collineatar perform?
e. What incentive was given to encourage French *francs-archers* to serve?
f. Who said, 'In all men there is an innate excitability and drive which is kindled by the heat of the fight, and it is the function of the general not to quench but to heighten that excitement.'?
g. Who commanded the English fleet that fought the Spanish Armada?

Answers 4

a. He was blind!

b. Pharsalus. 48 PC.

c. A type of shield.

d. The use of dismounted knights with longbowmen.

e. Sulphur, naptha or quicklime, or a combination of all three.

f. Xenophon.

g. The Earl of Warwick.

Answers 5

a. Alaric the Goth.

b. By 'friendly fire' – one of his cannon exploded at the siege of Roxburgh.

c. Adrianople, in 378 AD.

d. A notch cut in a shield into which a lance could be slotted for greater stability during a charge.

e. At Acre; they were siege engines.

f. A great storm, known as the *kamikaze* (Divine Wind).

g. Literally, 'sharpshooters'; units of *Streltsi* constituted the standing army and bodyguard of Ivan the Terrible.

Answers 6

a. Sir John Hawkwood.

b. It was a Jewish revolt against the Syrian occupation of Palestine in the second century BC.

c. Manzikert.

d. Battles.

e. A knight's warhorse.

f. Winchelsea.

g. An Ottoman Janissary regiment.

Answers 7

a. A Spartan general and admiral, whose cutting of the Athenian grain supply effectively led to Spartan victory in the Peloponnesian War.

b. Infantry withstood the attack of determined knights on horseback.

c. The pavise, a large shield.

d. He was responsible for firing a large handgun.

e. They were exempt from certain taxes.

f. Julius Caesar.

g. Lord Howard of Effingham.

Questions 8
a. Who killed one of his friends and leading subordinates after a drunken quarrel in the capital of Bactria?
b. How did the Battle of Losecoat Field (1470) gain its name?
c. Name the original Pyrrhic victory.
d. What was a castle-cat?
e. What did the term caracole mean?
f. What was unusual about Chinese Admiral Yi Sun-sin's 'Turtle Ships'?
g. Which army perfected fighting from a wagenburg?

Questions 9
a. Name the commander of the Greek forces at Thermopylae.
b. Mongol Subotai versus Hungarian King Bela IV (1241). Which battle?
c. What was a belfry?
d. What was a tercio?
e. Who was described by the French as 'the God-damn with his crooked stick'?
f. Who said, 'They make a desert and call it peace.'?
g. What did the Commission of Array allow an English king to do?

Questions 10
a. How did Mucius Scaevola come by his nickname 'the left-handed'?
b. Name the most successful Constable of France during the Hundred Years War.
c. Which Yorkist victory of the Wars of the Roses was won on Palm Sunday 1461?
d. What were virtons and dondaines?
e. What was the role of *adalides* in the Spanish army?
f. Who said: 'Few men are born brave; many become so through training and force of discipline.'?
g. What is the meaning of gleve?

Questions 11
a. Richard I of England was killed at the siege of which French castle?
b. At which battle was Hannibal finally defeated?
c. Which Swiss victory of 1315 was described as, 'not a battle, just a butchery of Duke Leopold's men'?
d. What was a *morgenstern* (morning star)?
e. What was the name of Alexander the Great's horse?
f. How did the Anglo-Irish horsemen hobilars gain their name?
g. Which two powers fought the Battle of Choggia in 1380?

Answers 8

a. Alexander the Great murdered Clitus at Bactra in 329 BC.

b. Fleeing rebels threw away their liveries to avoid recognition.

c. Heraclea, 280 BC.

d. A siege engine comprising tower and shed, the latter usually housing a battering ram.

e. A tactic supposedly used by Renaissance cavalry which involved them closing on an enemy, discharging their pistols and then retiring via the flanks to their own rear to reload before recommencing the tactic.

f. They were almost totally enclosed in wood, faced with iron sheets which sprouted metal spikes to defeat boarders.

g. The Hussites.

Answers 9

a. Leonidas, King of Sparta.

b. Mohi

c. A generic name given to siege towers.

d. A pike-and-shot block favoured by Spanish Renaissance armies.

e. An English archer.

f. Tacitus, in *The Agricola*.

g. Call out local militias.

Answers 10

a. He plunged his right hand into a fire to show that he was not afraid of torture when arrested on a mission to assassinate Lars Porsena, the Etruscan king.

b. Bertrand du Guesclin (1370–80).

c. Towton.

d. Types of crossbow bolt.

e. They acted as guides through enemy territory.

f. Flavius Vegetius Romanus.

g. A unit of troops usually found in middle and eastern Europe.

Answers 11

a. Chaluz (1199).

b. Zama.

c. Mortgarten.

d. A type of spiked club.

e. Bucephalus.

f. After the name of their mount, the hobby, Irish for 'nimble'.

g. The Venetian fleet defeated that of Genoa.

Questions 12
a. Who were massacred in Paris on St. Bartholomew's Day 1572?
b. Name three countries invaded by the Vandals.
c. Which battle of the Hundred Years War effectively lost Normandy for the English?
d. What was a rhomphaia?
e. What was a gambeson?
f. What, at least initially, reduced the manoeuvrability of the French fleet at Sluys (1340)?
g. What name was given to the units of the Swiss cantons?

Questions 13
a. Who commanded the Greek forces at Marathon (490 BC)?
b. Whose treachery at the Battle of Northampton (1460) led to a Yorkist victory?
c. Name the rival commanders at the Battle of Crecy (1346).
d. What was the 'Parthian shot'?
e. A hackbut was an early type of what?
f. Which city was known as 'The Red Apple' to the Ottomans?
g. What was a jinete?

Questions 14
a. Who was Perkin Warbeck alleged to be?
b. The siege of which city ended in disaster for the Athenians during the Peloponnesian War?
c. In which year did the Reconquista effectively end with the capture of Granada?
d. What was an arbalest?
e. How many centuries were in an imperial Roman cohort?
f. Of which type of soldier was it said that large groups are 'the most necessary thing in the world, for in small numbers they are useless'?
g. What animals were said to have saved Rome from the Gauls in 390 BC?

Questions 15
a. Who triumphed over Totila at the Battle of Taginae in 552 AD?
b. Who suffered three successive defeats against the Swiss in the Battles of Grandson (1476), Morat (1476) and Nancy (1477)?
c. Where in 73 AD did all the defenders commit suicide rather than surrender?
d. What were *meurtrieres*?
e. What was the meaning of the Irish term *buannacht*?
f. Who said, 'Soldiers usually estimate their prospects by the appearance of their general.'?
g. Name the three basic divisions of a Swiss army.

Answers 12

a. Protestants, many of whom had come to the city to celebrate the marriage of Henry of Navarre.

b. France, Spain, Algeria, Tunisia, Italy.

c. Formigny (1450).

d. A sinuously curved, long-bladed sword, much used by elements of the Byzantine army.

e. A quilted cloth jacket.

f. Parts of the fleet were chained together.

g. Banners.

Answers 13

a. Miltiades devised the plan that defeated the Persians. The formal commander-in-chief was Callimachus, who died in the battle.

b. Lord Grey.

c. Edward III of England and Philip VI of France.

d. A shot fired over the rear of his horse by a Parthian archer.

e. A handgun.

f. Constantinople.

g. A javelin-equipped Spanish light horseman.

Answers 14

a. Richard, Duke of York.

b. Syracuse.

c. 1492.

d. A type of crossbow with a steel bow spanned by mechanical means.

e. Six.

f. Longbowmen.

g. Geese, by raising the alarm when the Gauls almost surprised the defenders of the citadel.

Answers 15

a. The Byzantine commander Narses.

b. Charles the Bold of Burgundy.

c. Masada.

d. Holes in the ceilings of fortified places through which offensive devices could be dropped on any attackers.

e. The arrangement by which freemen were obliged to lodge and provision soldiers.

f. The Byzantine Emperor Maurice, in *The Strategikon*.

g. Vorhut (vanguard), Gewalthut (centre) and Nachhut (rearguard).

Questions 16

a. Which Athenian commander deserted to advise Spartan forces in the Peloponnesian War?

b. Name the English commander killed at the Battle of Castillon (1453).

c. Where were the French decisively defeated by the Habsburgs in 1525?

d. What was a garrot?

e. What were the main roles of horsemen known as corrours?

f. Who said, 'This very day must decide for us either a complete victory or an honourable death.'?

g. The militiamen of which French city wore red and blue livery?

Questions 17

a. Name the commanders of the Norse army slaughtered by Harold Godwinson's troops at Stamford Bridge in 1066.

b. Name the first major engagement of the Wars of the Roses.

c. Whose beard was metaphorically singed by Francis Drake in 1587?

d. What does the term *chevauchée* refer to?

e. What was scutage?

f. Who said, 'Another such victory over the Romans and we are undone.'?

g. Who founded the English Yeoman of the Guard in 1485?

Questions 18

a. Whose decisive intervention at Bosworth (1485) helped win the battle for Henry Tudor?

b. At what land battle in 479 BC were the Persians of Xerxes finally defeated in Greece?

c. Edward Baliol versus Donald, Earl of Mar (1332). Which battle?

d. Who or what was a peltast?

e. What was a gisarme?

f. What would a Roman naval captain do with a corvusl

g. What is the more common name of the Order of the Knights of the Church of St. Mary the Virgin?

Questions 19

a. Which Chinese dynasty built the Great Wall of China?

b. At which battle was Simon de Montfort killed?

c. What were the two main advantages that the crossbow had over the longbow?

d. And its two main disadvantages?

e. What was the origin of the term *condottieri*?

f. Whose epitaph was, 'Go tell the Spartans, thou who passest by, that here, obedient to their laws, we lie.'?

g. Whose banner featured a black porcupine on a white field?

Answers 16
a. Alcibiades.
b. Sir John Talbot, Earl of Shrewsbury.
c. At Pavia, in Italy. French monarch Francis I was captured.
d. A type of bolt/quarrel made of metal and wood.
e. Scouting, protecting the flanks and skirmishing.
f. Mark Anthony, before the first battle of Phillipi.
g. Paris.

Answers 17
a. Harald Hardrada and Tostig, Godwinson's brother.
b. St Albans (1455).
c. Philip II, King of Spain.
d. Literally a procession of horse, used to describe a deliberate campaign of wholesale destruction carried out by an army as it moved through enemy territory.
e. Payment made to avoid/in lieu of military service in England.
f. Pyrrhus.
g. Henry VII.

Answers 18
a. Sir William Stanley.
b. Plataea.
c. Dupplin Moor.
d. A Greek light infantryman of the 4th century BC, called after the small, round shield he carried.
e. A staff weapon topped by a crescent-shaped axe-head.
f. He would use it on enemy vessels; it was a spiked plank dropped onto ships to allow boarders to get to close quarters.
g. The Teutonic Knights.

Answers 19
a. The Han.
b. Evesham (1265).
c. Range and armour penetration.
d. Its rate of fire was much slower, and it was more expensive.
e. From the word *condotta*, the contract agreed between employer and mercenary leader.
f. The Spartans who died at Thermopylae in 480 BC.
g. Duc d'Orleans.

Questions 20
a. Name the English knight killed in single combat by Robert the Bruce before the Battle of Bannockburn (1314).
b. The Teutonic Knights were founded during which siege?
c. What battle allowed Saladin to recapture Jerusalem in 1187?
d. How did Archimedes hope to use the sun during the siege of Syracuse (212 BC)?
e. What was a falchion?
f. What is the origin of the word bombard?
g. Who were the White Hoods?

Questions 21
a. Who led Spanish armies in successful campaigns in the Netherlands but failed to link up with the Spanish Armada?
b. Who died after his defeat at Carrhae 53 BC?
c. What was unique about the Battle of Pilltown (1462)?
d. What were known to the Italians as *schioppettieri*?
e. What was a misericorde?
f. Who said, 'Therefore I say, "Know the enemy and know yourself: in a hundred battles you will never be in peril."'?
g. Whose troops wore the *clave signati*?

Questions 22
a. What was Lambert Simnel's fate after he was captured at Stoke Field (1487)?
b. Which battle sealed the fate of the Moors in Portugal?
c. In what tactical formation would a hoplite have preferred to fight?
d. What was bard?
e. What symbol was displayed to indicate that the Ottoman Sultan himself was in command of an army in the field?
f. Who, when advised that a course of action was difficult, said: 'We will either find a way or make one.'?
g. What did the term *landsknecht* mean?

Questions 23
a. Name the rival commanders at the Battle of Stirling Bridge (1297).
b. Henry V of England died after contracting dysentery during the siege of which town?
c. Name Alexander's three great victories over the Persians.
d. Where in a castle would one find a talus?
e. What, to the Crusaders, was Outremer?
f. Who said, '…such trifling causes as groundless suspicion, or sudden panic, or superstitious scruples frequently produce great disasters.'?
g. What was an aventail?

Answers 20
a. Sir Henry de Bohun.
b. Acre (1190).
c. Hattin.
d. He intended to reflect and concentrate the sun's rays with mirrors to burn the Roman siege engines.
e. A short, broad-bladed sword with one cutting edge.
f. From bombos, meaning a loud humming noise.
g. Troops raised in the Low Countries to combat the ravages of mercenary bands.

Answers 21
a. The Duke of Parma.
b. Crassus.
c. It was the only battle of the Wars of the Roses to take place in Ireland.
d. Handgunners.
e. A type of dagger, triangular in section with a single-edged blade.
f. Sun Tzu, in *The Art of War*.
g. The crossed keys were the badge of Papal forces.

Answers 22
a. He was put to work in Henry VII's kitchens.
b. Las Navas de Tolosa (1212).
c. A phalanx.
d. A set of horse armour.
e. Banners made of horses' tails.
f. Hannibal.
g. Literally, 'territorial' or 'national soldiers', referring specifically to mercenary units in the Renaissance period.

Answers 23
a. John de la Warenne, Earl of Surrey, and William Wallace.
b. Meaux (1421–22).
c. Issus, Granicus, Guagamela.
d. At the foot of a tower. It was a sloping section of brick/stone work designed to impede the progress of undermining.
e. The Christian kingdoms founded in and around Palestine.
f. Julius Caesar, in *The Civil War*.
g. A length of chain mail protecting the neck and shoulders.

Questions 24

a. Name the victor of the Battle of Lake Peipus (1242).

b. Name the hill defended by the Saxons at Hastings in 1066.

c. Name the battle of 1403 that saw the death of Henry Hotspur.

d. What was a glaive?

e. What was a chanfron?

f. Who said, 'An army of deer led by a lion is more to be feared than an army of lions led by a deer.'?

g. What were the roles of akincis in an Ottoman army?

Questions 25

a. Who commanded the Assyrians that came down 'like a wolf on the fold'?

b. Name the commander of the decisive English flank attack at Poitiers (1356).

c. Where did Boadicea wreak revenge upon the Romans for the ill-treatment of herself and her daughters?

d. What were letzinen?

e. Which warrior nation was decisively defeated at the Lechfeld in 955?

f. During the crossing of marshes just before the Battle of Lake Trasimene, what mishap befell Hannibal?

g. Who defeated whom at Mohácz in 1526?

Questions 26

a. Who won the Battle of the Milvian Bridge (312 AD)?

b. Name Owen Glendower's crushing victory over Edmund Mortimer in 1402.

c. What was a musculus?

d. By what name is the *bec-de-faucon* better known?

e. What were Marius' mules?

f. Who said, 'I will not demean myself by stealing victory like a thief.'?

g. Which Swiss cantons founded the Ever-Lasting League in 1291?

Questions 27

a. Name the leader of the French force that attacked the English baggage camp at Agincourt (1415).

b. What was the political significance of Caesar crossing the Rubicon?

c. Name Tamburlane's 1402 victory over Sultan Bayezit I.

d. What was a schiltron?

e. Name the three methods of imparting power to pre-gunpowder siege engines.

f. What tactic put the Spanish Armada to flight when it anchored in the Calais Roads?

g. Who were the *faux francais*?

Answers 24
a. Alexander Nevsky.
b. Senlac Hill.
c. Shrewsbury.
d. A pole-arm with a long cutting blade.
e. Armour covering the face of a horse.
f. Philip of Macedon (although the saying is sometimes attributed to Chabrias).
g. Light horsemen used for scouting, raiding and intelligence gathering.

Answers 25
a. Sennacherib.
b. Jean de Grailly, Captal de Buch.
c. At Colchester, London and St Albans, where she massacred the settlers.
d. Barriers of loose stones built by the Swiss to slow/disorder an enemy attack.
e. The Magyars, whose raids into Germany now ended.
f. He lost the sight of one eye.
g. The Ottoman army defeated Hungarian forces and occupied Hungary.

Answers 26
a. Constantine the Great.
b. Philleth (Bryn Glas).
c. Literally 'mouse', a bore for breaking through walls.
d. The Lucerne hammer.
e. Roman legionaries, so called because of the loads they had to carry.
f. Alexander the Great before the Battle of Arbela, when urged to make a night attack.
g. Uri, Schwyz and Unterwalden.

Answers 27
a. Clignet de Brabant.
b. The Rubicon river marked the boundary of Caesar's legal authority and, by crossing it to march on Rome, he was clearly signalling his intention to take power.
c. Ankara.
d. A densely-packed block of Scottish pikemen.
e. Torsion, tension and counterweight.
f. The English sent in fireships.
g. Frenchmen who fought for the English in the Hundred Years War.

Questions 28
a. Who did Alexander the Great name as his successor?
b. Name the three Christian commanders of the Third Crusade.
c. What is considered the first pitched land battle of the Hundred Years War?
d. What was a boulevard?
e. Why had the garrison of a besieged castle reason to fear a *malvoisin* (bad neighbour)?
f. How did Julius Caesar repay pirates who had held him to ransom while he was travelling to Rhodes?
g. Who led the Spanish force that conquered Inca Peru?

Questions 29
a. Who was Caesar's most implacable adversary during the conquest of Gaul?
b. At which battle of 1434 did the Bohemian League decisively defeat the Hussites?
c. What was an aketon?
d. What were 'London', 'Messenger' and 'The King's Daughter'?
e. What were pottes?
f. Of whom did Thucydides write, 'For they had learned that true safety was to be found in long previous training and not in eloquent exhortations uttered when they were going into action.'?
g. Which army adopted the St Andrew's cross in red and yellow as a field recognition device?

Questions 30
a. Which Mongol leader was known as 'The Lame'?
b. Name the rival commanders at Bannockburn (1314).
c. Varro versus Hannibal (216 BC). Which battle?
d. What was the only type of medieval siege engine not based on Greek or Roman design?
e. What was peytral?
f. Name the two-day naval battle of 1372 that saw the annihilation of the English fleet.
g. From what wood was an English longbow made?

Questions 31
a. Name the rival forces that fought at the Battle of Wisby (1361).
b. After what battle did Brutus commit suicide?
c. What was a *mortel-de-fer*?
d. In what important technical respect were Roman cavalry inferior to medieval knights?
e. How did Hannibal find out that his brother Hasdrubal, bringing Carthaginian reinforcements into Italy, had been defeated by the Romans in 207 BC?
f. Whose deathbed advice to his sons was, 'Give the soldiers money and despise everyone else.'?
g. Constable Charles d'Albert led French forces to disaster at which battle?

Answers 28
a. Perdiccas.
b. Richard I, Frederick I (Barbarossa), and Philip I.
c. Morlaix (1342).
d. A type of earthwork, one usually mounting artillery.
e. It was a type of assault tower which enabled attackers to fire down on the defenders.
f. As soon as his ransom was paid, he commandeered vessels from Miletus, followed and captured the pirates and had them crucified at Pergamum.
g. Pissarro.

Answers 29
a. Vercingetorix.
b. Lipassy.
c. A padded jacket often worn under armour.
d. Three English cannon at the 1415 siege of Harfleur.
e. Holes in the ground, dug to break up cavalry charges.
f. The Spartans at the Battle of Mantinea, 428 BC.
g. The Burgundian.

Answers 30
a. Timur-i-Leng (Tamburlane).
b. Edward II of England and Robert the Bruce of Scotland.
c. Cannae.
d. The trebuchet – it worked on the counterweight principle, unknown in the Ancient World.
e. Armour covering a horse's chest.
f. La Rochelle.
g. Yew – mainly imported from Italy and Spain.

Answers 31
a. Danes and Gotlanders.
b. Philippi.
c. A long-shafted war hammer.
d. They did not have stirrups.
e. Hasdrubal's severed head was catapulted into the Carthaginian camp.
f. The Emperor Septimius Severus, 211 AD.
g. Agincourt, 1415.

Questions 32
a. Who was the Persian king defeated by Alexander the Great?
b. Name the rival commanders at the Battle of Lewes (1264).
c. At which battle were the Teutonic Knights virtually annihilated?
d. After what piece of equipment was Caligula called?
e. What is the literal meaning of the name Genghis Khan?
f. After which battle were the Flemish dead described as being 'slain by heaps, one upon the other'?
g. Who created the English Order of the Garter?

Questions 33
a. Who led the Roman troops that invaded Scotland in 79 AD?
b. Who was Lambert Simnel alleged to be?
c. At which two battles of 1461 in the Wars of the Roses did snowstorms affect the outcome?
d. What was a *langue-de-boeuf* (ox-tongue)?
e. Name the two most common ways of reloading a crossbow.
f. How many cohorts were in an imperial legion?
g. Which units contained the following ranks: Chief Soup-maker and Chief Cook?

Questions 34
a. Who led the army that Horatio and two companions defied on the bridge to Rome?
b. Name the Black Prince's great Spanish victory of 1367.
c. What innovation did the Bureau brothers, Gaspard and Jean, bring to French armies of the Hundred Years War?
d. Where did Charles Martel defeat Islamic forces in 732?
e. What was a gallowglass (*galloglaich*)?
f. Who said, 'Why lose men, even for victory?... Victory through policy is as much a mark of the good general as victory by the sword.'?
g. What was a jupon?

Questions 35
a. Whose death did Achilles avenge by killing Hector?
b. Poitiers (1356) saw the demise of which French order of chivalry?
c. What is considered the bloodiest battle to have been fought on English soil?
d. What was a gladius?
e. What was the largest sea battle of the Ancient World?
f. What were *provisionati* in Italian armies?
g. What was the Clos de Galees?

Answers 32
a. Darius.
b. Simon de Montfort and Henry III.
c. Tannenberg (1410).
d. Army boots.
e. Great/Universal Lord.
f. Roosebeke (1382).
g. Edward III.

Answers 33
a. Agricola.
b. Edward, Earl of Warwick.
c. Second St Albans and Towton.
d. A type of pole-arm with a dagger-like blade.
e. By stirrup or windlass.
f. Ten.
g. The Janissaries.

Answers 34
a. Lars Porsena.
b. Navarette.
c. An effective artillery train.
d. Poitiers.
e. An Irish/mercenary heavy infantryman dressed in armour and equipped, usually, with a long-shafted axe.
f. Julius Caesar, in *The Civil War*.
g. A tight fitting coat worn over armour.

Answers 35
a. Patroclus.
b. The Order of the Star.
c. Towton (1461).
d. A Roman short sword.
e. Actium 31 BC.
f. Regularly waged, permanently employed troops.
g. A French naval base/arsenal situated near Rouen.

Questions 36
a. Who was 'the delayer'?
b. Robert the Bruce versus Aymer de Valence, Duke of Pembroke. Which battle of 1307?
c. What great city was taken and sacked in 1099?
d. What was the name of the circular handguard found on tournament lances?
e. Who were the 'Sea Beggars'?
f. Of whom did the King of France say, 'Kill me those scoundrels, for they block our advance and serve no purpose.'?
g. From 1309, where was the headquarters of the Teutonic Knights?

Questions 37
a. Under which Emperor did the Roman Empire reach its greatest extent?
b. After which battle of the Wars of the Roses was Owen Tudor executed?
c. What battle formation was described as *en herce*?
d. What was a goat?
e. What was the official name of France's senior field commanders of the Hundred Years War?
f. Who advised, 'Do not thwart an enemy returning home ... Do not press an enemy at bay.'?
g. What was a kern?

Questions 38
a. Who ran the original marathon?
b. Who commanded the Yorkist right wing at Barnet (1471)?
c. Name the only major battle of the Third Crusade.
d. What was a *Schweizergegen*?
e. What special responsibility did an *aquilifer* have?
f. What was a dromon?
g. Where would you find crenels and merlons?

Questions 39
a. Whose 10,000 escaped from Persia in 400 BC?
b. How did Alexander take the sea port of Tyre in 332 BC?
c. What type of castle is described as a *gran Bugue* (great ship)?
d. What was a tabur?
e. Who first established the Royal Navy?
f. At which English battle of 1387 did one commentator state, 'Scarce ten ounces of blood was lost on both sides.'?
g. Name the red banner from the Abbey St. Denis carried at, among other battles, Agincourt.

Answers 36
a. Fabius 'Cunctator'.
b. Loudon Hill.
c. Jerusalem, by the army of the First Crusade.
d. Vamplate.
e. Dutch privateers in small vessels who fought against the Spanish during the 16th century.
f. The Genoese crossbowmen at Crecy (1346).
g. Marienberg.

Answers 37
a. Trajan, who came to power in 98 AD.
b. Mortimer's Cross (1461).
c. The wedge formation of English longbowmen.
d. A timber structure with ropes and pulleys used to lift cannon from their travelling carriages onto their battle mounts.
e. Constable, a corruption of Count of the Stable.
f. Sun Tzu, in *The Art of War*.
g. A lightly-equipped Irish foot soldier.

Answers 38
a. Pheidippedes.
b. Richard, Duke of Gloucester, later Richard III.
c. Arsuf (1191).
d. A wooden-handled short sword associated with the Swiss.
e. Looking after the standard of a Roman legion.
f. A Roman warship.
g. They are parts of a castle's battlements.

Answers 39
a. Xenophon led 10,000 Greek mercenaries back to safety.
b. Tyre was an island; Alexander built a causeway out to it, and led a successful assault along the causeway.
c. One with a long and narrow, ship-like ground plan.
d. An Ottoman field fortification comprising carts chained together.
e. Alfred the Great, who raised a fleet that defeated the Danes at the River Lea in 895.
f. Radcot Bridge.
g. The *Oriflamme*; though this means 'Golden Flame', it was red.

Questions 40
a. In what country did Hannibal die?
b. What was 'Greek Fire'?
c. What was a brattice?
d. What was the basis of England's Livery and Maintenance System?
e. What were *phalerae*?
f. Who said, 'Carthage must be destroyed.'?
g. Why did the Emperor Augustus ask on his deathbed, 'Where are my Eagles?'?

Questions 41
a. Name the blind Hussite commander who won victories at Skalice and Malesov in 1424.
b. In what part of Europe did Emperor Marcus Aurelius order a legion to be decimated?
c. 'You hear that X goes where he pleases not by marching his phalanx of infantry, but by bringing in his train light infantry, cavalry, archers, mercenaries and other such troops.' Who was the X whose combined-arms tactics Demosthenes was describing?
d. What was a sarissa?
e. Who were nicknamed 'skinners'?
f. Who recommended leaving a 'golden bridge' for a fleeing enemy?
g. What was a barbute?

Answers 40

a. He took poison in Bithynia.

b. An inflammable mixture, mainly consisting of naptha and launched by catapult.

c. A wooden structure that jutted out over a castle's battlements to command the base of a wall.

d. Troops would fight in the livery of a lord in return for his protection.

e. Roman campaign medals.

f. Cato the Elder.

g. Three Roman legions had been destroyed by German tribes of the Teutoburgerwald in 9 AD. The disaster haunted Augustus until his death 5 years later.

Answers 41

a. Jan Zizka.

b. In Dacia, in the Danube valley, where he spent much of his reign campaigning against the Marcommani and Quadi.

c. Philip of Macedon.

d. A long pike used by Greek, particularly Macedonian, troops.

e. Members of the Free Companies.

f. Scipio Africanus.

g. An open-faced helmet of Italian origin.

1600 – 1914

Questions 1

a. Which Confederate commander was dubbed the 'King of Spades'?
b. Who led the relief force to Kandahar in the Afghan War of 1879–80?
c. Where did 'Thornhill's Roughs' (also known as the 'Carving Knife Brigade') gain fame?
d. Where did Napoleon first employ his 'lozenge' attacking formation?
e. Which Union ironclad monitor was sunk at the Battle of Hampton Roads?
f. Who said, 'The object of artillery should not consist of killing men on the whole of the enemy's front but to overthrow it, to destroy parts of this front... then they obtain decisive results; they make a gap.'?
g. Who, in 1902, said, 'We are a bloody cheerful-looking lot of British subjects.'?

Questions 2

a. Who was the first commander of the New Model Army?
b. Name the position at First Bull Run/Mannasas where Stonewall Jackson earned his nickname.
c. When was the Battle of Sedgemoor?
d. What was a *razzia* as devised by French officer Bugeard in Algeria in the 1840s?
e. Which Napoleonic marshal sat on the touch-hole of an Austrian cannon to prevent the destruction of the Danube bridge at Spitz in 1805?
f. President Abraham Lincoln's remark, 'I can't spare this man. He fights', concerned which Union general?
g. Who were known as Sarps in the Second Anglo-Boer War?

Questions 3

a. Which general fought for both American and Polish independence?
b. Which Confederate general ended his days as president of the Georgia Military Academy?
c. Surveying the carnage of which battle did Napoleon remark, '*Cest le plus beau champs de bataille que j'ai encore vu*' ('It's the most beautiful battlefield that I have ever seen').?
d. Why are the apprentice boys of Londonderry so feted by Northern Irish Protestants?
e. What did the Boer term *kriegsraad* mean?
f. Who said, 'In war, the moral is to the material as three is to one.'?
g. Who said, 'General Lee, I have no division.'?

Answers 1

a. Robert E Lee.

b. Sir Frederick Roberts.

c. Defending the foreign legations in Peking during the Boxer Rebellion (1900).

d. Wagram (1809).

e. The *Tecumseh.*

f. The Comte de Guibert, the great French artillery reformer in his 1773 work, *Essai general de tactique.*

g Boer General Jacobus De La Rey.

Answers 2

a. Sir Thomas Fairfax, appointed in February 1645.

b. Henry House Hill.

c. 6 July 1685.

d. Separate columns converging on a single objective; an early form of search and destroy.

e. Marshal Lannes, trying to persuade the Austrians that there was an armistice and they should not destroy the bridge. He was successful in his ruse, and the bridge was taken intact.

f. General Ulysses S Grant.

g. The South African Police (from their shoulder-titles, SAAP, standing for South Africa Armed Police).

Answers 3

a. Tadeusz Kosciuszko: his services in the American War of Independence included building the fortress of West Point, and he was made a Brigadier-General in 1783. In Poland, he led the unsuccessful rising of 1794.

b. General Daniel Harvey Hill.

c. Borodino (1812).

d. They closed the gates of the town before Catholic forces could enter in 1689.

e. A meeting of heads of commandos to discuss tactics before a battle.

f. Napoleon.

g. General George Pickett at Gettysburg.

Questions 4

a. The death of which general was celebrated by Jacobites when toasting 'the little gentleman in black velvet'?

b. Who was successful with the 21st Lancers at Omdurman but lost an election the following year?

c. In the 17th century, what was King Philip's War?

d. What was the fate of Breaker Morant in the Second Anglo-Boer War?

e. Who, when asked what he would do if the British Army ever invaded Germany, is reported to have replied, 'Send a policeman along to arrest it.'?

f. Whose toast was, 'Our country! In her intercourse with foreign nations may she always be right, but our country, right or wrong!'?

g. Which British cavalry regiment was known as the 'Cherrypickers'?

Questions 5

a. Which French commander was wounded at Malplaquet but led his men in person to storm the entrenchments at Denain in 1712?

b. Name Britain's reforming Secretary of State for War appointed in 1868.

c. What conflict was described as 'not a war at all – just a street row'?

d. What type of weapon was a Maori *patiti*?

e. Which Union general's horse was called 'Rienzi'?

f. Who said, 'We come to give you liberty and equality but don't lose your heads about it – the first person who stirs without permission will be shot.'?

g. Alabama Red Rovers and New Orleans Greys. Which army?

Questions 6

a. Who died at Sans Souci?

b. Name the commander of the Rorke's Drift garrison (1879).

c. Name the two Confederate forts that protected Mobile Bay.

d. What type of weapon was a jingal?

e. Who did Union General Grant describe as, 'the most conspicuous figure who did not exercise a separate command'?

f. About which general did George II remark, 'Mad is he? Then I hope he will bite some of my other generals.'?

g. Orange and red sashes distinguished what at Edgehill in 1642?

Questions 7

a. Name the officer in charge of the infamous Confederate prisoner of war camp at Andersonville.

b. Name the first outright French victory of the Franco-Prussian War.

c. Name the fortress defended by Orman Pasha in 1877.

d. Name the Union warship sunk by a Confederate submarine in 1864.

e. Why were Indian mutineers executed by being blown from the ends of cannon?

f. Who said, 'The village of Fuentes de Onoro, having been the field of battle, has not been much improved by the circumstance.'?

g. What is the origin of the grey and white uniform worn by cadets at the US Military Academy at West Point?

Answers 4
a. William III – William of Orange, who supplanted James II on the throne of England. William died after being thrown when his horse stumbled over a mole hill.
b. Winston Churchill.
c. A war between Indians and settlers in New England, 1675–78. 'King Philip' was the principal Indian leader involved.
d. He was executed for the murder of Boer prisoners.
e. Count Otto von Bismarck.
f. American naval officer Stephen Decatur.
g. The 11th Hussars, because of their cherry-red trousers.

Answers 5
a. Marshal Villars.
b. Lord Cardwell.
c. The Anglo-Burmese War of 1885.
d. A short tomahawk.
e. General Phil Sheridan.
f. General (later Marshal) Lefebvre during the French Revolutionary wars, on occupying Königsberg.
g. The Texan Army during the War of Independence.

Answers 6
a. Frederick the Great. Sans Souci was his palace at Potsdam.
b. Lieutenant JRM Chard, Royal Engineers.
c. Forts Gaines and Morgan.
d. A heavy matchlock usually supported on a tripod/bipod.
e. Union General Winfield Scott Hancock.
f. General James Wolfe.
g. Orange sashes were worn by Essex's parliamentarians, while the King's forces wore red sashes.

Answers 7
a. Henry Wirtz.
b. Coulmiers (9 November 1870).
c. Plevna.
d. The *Housatonic*, sunk by the submarine H L Huntley.
e. It instilled fear, as the sepoys believed that they would not be able to enter heaven if their bodies were not whole.
f. The Duke of Wellington, in a dispatch of May 1811.
g. During the Anglo-American War of 1812–15, one brigade of regulars went into action without regulation uniforms. They were dressed in short, light grey jackets and white trousers, which became the uniform worn by West Point cadets.

Questions 8
a. Which commander at Waterloo was known as 'Old Forwards'?
b. What was the native American name for General-President Andrew Jackson?
c. Simon Bolivar's victory at Carabobo (1821) effectively secured die independence of which South American country?
d. By what name are Maxim-Nordenfeldt guns better known?
e. Who said, 'Perhaps I should not insist on this bold manoeuvre, but it is my style, my way of doing things.'?
f. On which memorial do the following words appear, 'Life, sooner than courage, forsook these soldiers of France.'?
g. Which army contained units called Dark Sheep, Unfeeling Devourers and Mongrels?

Questions 9
a. Who were the two military leaders who revolutionised tactics during the early 17th century?
b. Whose murder in Kabul led to the Afghan War of 1879–80?
c. Sam Houston's retreat from Gonzales to Harrisburg during the Texan War of Independence was nicknamed what?
d. Name Nelson's flagship at the Battle of the Nile (1798).
e. For what is Union General Lew Wallace perhaps best known?
f. Of what did Napoleon say, 'I take greater pleasure in this reading than a young lady would get from reading a novel.'?
g. What rank was held by a havildar?

Questions 10
a. Who commanded the French forces at Blenheim in 1704?
b. In the Crimea, what relation was Lord Cardigan to Lord Lucan?
c. Name the four main battles of the American Civil War Seven Days' Campaign.
d. Admiral Wilhelm von Tegetthoff versus Count Carlo Pellion de Persano (1866). Which battle?
e. In the decade before seeing service in the Second Anglo-Boer War, General Warren was London's Police Commissioner. What was his most famous case?
f. Who said, 'The commanders of armies are more to be pitied than one would think ... yet of the thousands who condemn them, there is not one that could command even the smallest unit.'?
g. What were Burmese dacoits, faced by English troops in the late 19th century?

Questions 11
a. Who was the last of Napoleon's 1804 Marshals to die?
b. What role did Thaddeus Lowe fulfil for the North in the American Civil War?
c. The Battle of Chiao-tau took place in which war?
d. What was unusual about the weapon known as a fusil lance?
e. Which Confederate general said, 'I never like to go into battle with one boot off.'?
f. Who said, 'Our country will, I believe, sooner forgive an officer for attacking an enemy than for leaving it (sic) alone.'?
g. What was the meaning of a symbolic hand painted on a Sioux warrior's body?

Answers 8

a. Blucher – *Alte Vorwarts*.

b. Sharp Knife.

c. Venezuela.

d. Pom-poms.

e. Napoleon, in a letter to Prince Eugene in 1813.

f. One dedicated to the French Legionnaires who fought at the Battle of Camerone (Mexico) (1863).

g. The Zulu Army.

Answers 9

a. Prince Maurice of Nassau and Gustavus Adolphus.

b. Sir Louis Cavagnari.

c. The 'Runaway Scrape'.

d. HMS *Vanguard*.

e. He was the author of *Ben Hur*.

f. The twenty volumes he was sent every month updating the state of all his units; he usually spent an hour or two every day reading them.

g. Sergeant in the British-Indian Army.

Answers 10

a. Camille, Comte de Tallard.

b. Brother-in-law.

c. Mechanicsville, Gaines' Mill, Frayser's Farm and Malvern Hill.

d. Lissa.

e. Jack the Ripper.

f. Frederick the Great.

g. Bandits and renegades.

Answers 11

a. Nicolas-Jean de Dieu Soult, Duc de Dalmatie, in 1851.

b. He organised the observation balloon corps.

c. The Russo-Japanese War (1904–05).

d. It was a carbine that, by attaching a large bayonet, could be used as a lance.

e. General James Longstreet.

f. Nelson, during the attack on Bastia (May 1794).

g. He had killed a man in hand-to-hand combat.

Questions 12
a. What role did Erastus 'Deaf' Smith perform for the Texans during the War of Independence?
b. What was Herbert Kitchener's official title during the Omdurman campaign?
c. Which Southern city in the American Civil War was protected by the Dimmock Line?
d. What, in the Imperial Russian Navy, was an *ekipazh*?
e. What was the grog ration in Wellington's Peninsular Army?
f. Who said, 'Grant stood by me when I was crazy, and I stood by him when he was drunk.'?
g. What type of individuals filled the ranks of France's *Garde Mobile* during the Franco-Prussian War?

Questions 13
a. Which of Napoleon's marshals died after falling from a window on 1 June 1815, possibly not by accident?
b. Which great 17th century commander was killed by the English mercenary Walter Devereux?
c. Name Colonel Evelyn Wood's major victory over the Zulus.
d. What type of weapon was the American Civil War 'Covered Bridge Gun'?
e. Name the designer of the USS *Monitor*.
f. Who, on what occasion, said, 'Here goes the last of the Brudenells.'?
g. Who said, 'Money is dear; human life still dearer, but time is dearest of all.'?

Questions 14
a. Which US general was known as 'Old Rough and Ready'?
b. What was the last battle fought on English soil?
c. Name the Boer victory over the Zulus in 1838.
d. Name the rifle used by British foot regiments of the late 1870s in the Zulu War.
e. What was known to Confederate troops as the 'Virginia quickstep'?
f. Who said to whom, 'Activity, activity, speed!'?
g. What was the *levée en masse*?

Questions 15
a. Which Austrian general, who later drove the French out of Italy, was refused permission to enter the French army as a young man?
b. Who are said to have held the following conversation: 'By God, I've lost my leg, sir.' 'By God sir, so you have.' ?
c. Which 'battle' is considered to mark the end of the wars against the Native Americans?
d. By what name was the Confederate ironclad *Merrimac* known in the South?
e. Who said of what, 'I had it from Xenophon, but our friends here are astonished at what I have done, for they have read nothing.'?
f. At which American Civil War battle did Lee say: 'It is as well that war is so terrible; men would love it too much'?
g. What was unique about the French La Brigade des Drapeaux during the siege of Paris (1870–71)?

Answers 12
a. He acted as a guide and spy for Sam Houston.
b. Sirdar of the Egyptian Army.
c. Petersburg.
d. The basic permanent organisational unit.
e. 1/3 pint rum or 1 pint of wine per day. Gin often replaced rum.
f. General William T Sherman.
g. Men of military age who had been exempt from conscription.

Answers 13
a. Marshal Louis Alexandre Berthier.
b. Wallenstein. Devereux, who ran his commander through with a halberd, was part of a gang of English, Scots and Irish mercenaries who murdered the German general, almost certainly on the orders of Emperor Ferdinand.
c. Khambula (March 1879).
d. A type of multi-barrelled volley gun.
e. Swede John Ericsson.
f. General James Brudenell, Earl Cardigan, shortly before the Charge of the Light Brigade, October 1854.
g. Field Marshal Aleksander Suvorov.

Answers 14
a. General Zachary Taylor.
b. Clifton Moor, 18 December 1745, during the Jacobite Rebellion.
c. Blood River.
d. The Martini-Henry.
e. Diarrhoea.
f. Napoleon to Massena, April 1809, before the Battle of Eckmuhl.
g. Mass conscription in France during the Revolutionary Wars.

Answers 15
a. Prince Eugene. The son of the Comte de Soissons, his father was disgraced and the young man was not allowed to enter the French army. He was given a regiment in the Austrian army in 1683.
b. Henry Paget, Earl of Uxbridge, and Wellington, at Waterloo, where Paget commanded the British cavalry.
c. The massacre at Wounded Knee (December 1890).
d. The *Virginia*.
e. Brigadier General James Wolfe at the siege of Louisburg in 1758, explaining the inspiration behind his use of light infantry to force the French back into the fortress.
f. Fredericksburg.
g. It was the only regular army unit to serve in the capital's defence.

Questions 16
a. Which English general was the subject of a French popular song?
b. Who marched to the sound of the guns and died at the head of the cavalry charge that saved the day at Marengo (1800)?
c. Name the Northwest Frontier fort relieved by Lieutenant-Colonel J G Kelly in 1895.
d. What was the nickname of the Ager 'machine gun' of the American Civil War?
e. What did the word dervish signify?
f. Who did Charles I dismiss with the words, 'Seek your subsistence beyond the seas, to which end I send you a pass.'?
g. Who was the first black soldier to win the US Congressional Medal of Honor?

Questions 17
a. At which siege did Napoleon and Nelson fight on opposite sides?
b. Who commanded The Ever-Victorious Army (1863–64)?
c. What advance in ballistics was made by French Colonel de Beaulieu in the 1840s?
d. What was unique about the clash between the warships *Le Bouvet* and *Meteor* off Cuba in the early 1870s?
e. Who said, 'Well, if I am to become a doctor you must at least make Gneisenau an apothecary ... Gneisenau makes the pills that I administer.'?
f. Who replied to a questioner, 'All soldiers run away, madam.'?
g. Who call themselves 'Pontius Pilot's Bodyguard'?

Questions 18
a. Who was 'Bonnie Dundee'?
b. What role did French-Canadian Royal Engineer Eduard Girouard perform in Kitchener's Sudan campaign (1896–98)?
c. The Battle of Maipu (1818) secured the independence of which South American country?
d. Which Union warship was responsible for sinking the Confederate commerce-raider *Alabama*?
e. Who said, 'In audacity and obstinacy will be found safety.'?
f. Who said, 'You know, Foley, I have only one eye – I have a right to be blind sometimes. I really do not see the signal.'?
g. What were described as, 'Musketeers mounted, who serve sometimes a-foot, sometimes a-horseback, being always ready upon anything that requires expedition.'?

Questions 19
a. Who conducted 53 sieges and built 33 fortresses for Louis XIV?
b. Name the Russian commander-in-chief for most of the Crimean War.
c. On which American Civil War battlefield would you find Marye's Heights?
d. Which infamous episode of the Indian Mutiny occurred at Cawnpore's Bibighur (House of Women)?
e. What type of weapon was a dak?
f. Who said, 'Rangers of Connaught! It is not my intention to expend any powder this evening. We'll do this business with cold steel.'?
g. On what occasion did Robert E Lee say, 'I would rather die a thousand times.'?

Answers 16
a. Marlborough – *Malbruck s'en vat en guerre.*
b. Desaix.
c. Chitral.
d. The 'Coffee Mill'.
e. A Muslim vowed to poverty.
f. Prince Rupert of the Rhine.
g. William Carney, Fort Wagner, July 1863.

Answers 17
a. Toulon (1794).
b. Major Charles Gordon (later of Khartoum).
c. An early form of rifling for muzzle-loading cannon.
d. It was the only naval engagement of the Franco-Prussian War.
e. Blücher, in accepting an honorary doctorate at Oxford University after the Battle of Waterloo.
f. The Duke of Wellington, when asked whether British soldiers ever ran away.
g. The British 1st (or Royal) Regiment of Foot, in a reference to their longevity (they were raised in 1625).

Answers 18
a. Graham Claverhouse, Marquis of Montrose, who led small forces in Scotland on the Royalist side during the English Civil Wars. He was betrayed and hanged in May 1650.
b. He oversaw the building of the Sudan Military Railway.
c. Chile.
d. The *Kearsarge.*
e. Napoleon.
f. Nelson at the Battle of Copenhagen (2 April 1801), as recorded by Colonel William Parker.
g. Dragoons, in a 1702 Military Dictionary.

Answers 19
a. Marshal de Vauban, Louis XIV's great military engineer.
b. Prince Alexander Menshikov.
c. Fredericksburg.
d. The massacre of English women and children by the mutineers.
e. A Burmese sword.
f. Sir Thomas Picton, April 1812. He was addressing the 88th Foot just before the attack on Badajoz.
g. On going to discuss surrender terms at Appomattox Court House.

Questions 20
a. Who was von Seydlitz?
b. Who had overall command of the relief force during the attempt to reach Gordon at Khartoum?
c. Which action of the American Civil War was known as the 'Battle above the Clouds'?
d. Who was mastermind behind the Union's naval blockade of Southern ports known as the 'Anaconda Plan'?
e. What society did the Chinese Boxers belong to?
f. Who said, 'In siege warfare, as in the open field, it is the gun which plays the chief part... It is with artillery that war is made.'?
g. What type of troops were Sudanese *jihadiyya*?

Questions 21
a. At the Battle of Breitenfeld (1631), which imperial commander of 5000 cavalry charged the Swedish forces seven times but was ultimately defeated?
b. Which Boer commander was forced to surrender at Paardeberg Drift on the Modder River in 1900?
c. By what name is the Battle of Angostura, fought during the Mexican-American War, better known?
d. Who invented shrapnel?
e. What was the military significance of the Spanish tune called the *Deguello*?
f. Which Confederate officer spoke the following words, 'Go back. Do your duty, as I've done mine. I would rather die than be whipped.'?
g. What colour marked a Chinese Boxer's alliegance?

Questions 22
a. Whose forces massacred the defenders of Drogheda and Wexford?
b. Which great general had cello music written for him by Johann Christian Bach?
c. Name the French base camp during the Crimean War.
d. Name Union Flag Officer Samuel DuPont's victory of November 1861.
e. What did Marshal Jourdan lose (apart from the battle) at Vittoria (1813)?
f. Who, outside Ladysmith, said, 'When God holds out a finger, do not take the whole hand'?
g. Who or what in the English Civil War were *reformados*?

Questions 23
a. Which marshal of France lost an eye to an accidental shot discharged by the Emperor Napoleon during a hunting expedition?
b. Who commanded the British troops that burnt Washington in 1814?
c. The Battle of Beecher's Island (1868) saw the death of which Cheyenne war leader?
d. Who was said to have sent the message '*peccavi*' ('I have sinned') in 1843?
e. What ruse did George Washington use to confuse British troops who had him pinned against the Delaware after the Battle of Trenton in 1778?
f. Of which Confederate commander did Sherman say, 'He had a genius for strategy which was original and, to me, incomprehensible.'?
g. What was a reiter?

Answers 20

a. Frederick the Great's cavalry commander during the Seven Years War.

b. Sir Garnet Wolseley.

c. Missionary Ridge-Lookout Mountain (November 1863).

d. General Winfield Scott.

e. The Righteous Harmonious Fists.

f. Napoleon after the Battle of Loebau (1809).

g. Riflemen.

Answers 21

a. Pappenheim.

b. General Cronje.

c. Buena Vista.

d. British General Henry Shrapnel. His spherical canister shell gave artillery a devastating new power, but he never felt that he was given sufficient material recompense for his invention.

e. It announced that no quarter would be given.

f. General JEB Stuart.

g. Red.

Answers 22

a. Oliver Cromwell, in 1649.

b. Frederick the Great.

c. Kamish.

d. Port Royal.

e. His marshal's baton – he dropped it during the precipitate French retreat.

f. Commandant-General Petrus Joubert.

g. Royalist cavalry officers fighting as private troopers because their commands had ceased to exist.

Answers 23

a. Andre Masséna, Duc de Rivoli, Prince d'Essling. Napoleon blamed Berthier!

b. General Robert Ross. The British fleet that landed them was commanded by Admiral Alexander Cochrane,

c. Roman Nose.

d. Charles Napier, after his conquest of the Sind in India.

e. He left his campfires burning and slipped round to attack them in the rear.

f. Nathan Bedford Forrest.

g. A 16th century German mercenary.

Questions 24
a. Name the Texan commander at San Jacinto.
b. Which British general twice saved Madras and resigned his command in between?
c. Graf Helmut von Moltke versus General Benedek (1866). Which battle?
d. What, in the American Civil War, were 'Ketcham's' and 'Haynes Excelsior'?
e. Who said, 'If I owned both Hell and Texas, I'd rent out Texas and live in Hell'?
f. Which force was 'killed out as hardly any army had been killed out in the history of war'?
g. Which English Civil War commander dressed his regiment in purple?

Questions 25
a. Who was known as 'Black Dick'?
b. Name the ill-fated garrison commander of Cawnpore during the Indian Mutiny.
c. Which clash of the American Civil War was precipitated by a Confederate raid to capture shoes?
d. What weapon was known to the Maoris as the 'duck's bill'?
e. Who wrote, 'Everything in war is very simple, but the simplest thing is very difficult.'?
f. Of which Union commander did Lincoln state, 'Only X (could) snatch defeat from the jaws of victory.'?
g. In which 'army' would you have found the Californian Rangers Revolver Brigade and the American First Rifle Brigade?

Questions 26
a. Which black general defied Napoleon's armies in Haiti and had himself proclaimed Emperor?
b. Which US general was known as 'Old Fuss and Feathers'?
c. Which 'army' was decisively defeated at Trout River, Canada, in 1870?
d. By what name is the Mission of San Antonio de Valero better known?
e. What was the 'Needle Gun'?
f. Who said, 'Let us have a respectable army and such as will be competent to every contingency.'?
g. About which disaster did Queen Victoria say, 'The Government alone is to blame.'?

Questions 27
a. Which English Civil War general always carried his own winding sheet with him on campaign?
b. Who became British commander-in-chief in India in July 1857?
c. What were the Lines of Torres Vedras?
d. Who was the first American to hold the rank of Rear-Admiral?
e. How did Napoleon get his nickname 'the little corporal'?
f. Who said at the First Battle of Bull Run (1861), 'There stands Jackson like a stone wall.'?
g. What item of wear was a havelock?

Answers 24

a. General Sam Houston.

b. Sir Eyre Coote. He defeated the French under Lally at Wandewash in 1759, resigned as C-in-C of Madras' forces in 1769, but was recalled to India in 1779 and defeated Hyder Ali's forces threatening Madras at Porto Novo in 1781.

c. Königgratz/Sadowa.

d. Hand grenades.

e. Phil Sheridan.

f. The Dervish Army at Omdurman (1898).

g. Lord Brooke, a Parliamentarian who died at Lichfield in 1643.

Answers 25

a. Admiral Lord Howe (1726–99), because of his swarthy complexion.

b. General Sir Hugh Wheeler.

c. Gettysburg.

d. The Brown Bess musket.

e. Karl von Clausewitz (*On War*).

f. General Ambrose Burnside.

g. The 'digger' army at the Eureka Stockade (1854).

Answers 26

a. Jean Jacques Dessalines, who succeeded Toussaint L'Ouverture when the latter was betrayed to the French in 1803.

b. General Winfield Scott.

c. The Fenian Brotherhood led by Colonel John O'Neill.

d. The Alamo.

e. The breech-loader used by Prussian infantry during the Austro-Prussian and Franco-Prussian wars.

f. George Washington.

g. The fall of Khartoum and death of Gordon (1885).

Answers 27

a. The Earl of Essex.

b. Sir Colin Campbell.

c. Wellington's defensive line covering Lisbon during the Peninsular War.

d. David Glasgow Farragut.

e. By leading personally the critical bayonet charge across the bridge at the Battle of Lodi in 1796 – his troops were impressed both by his short stature and by his personal courage.

f. General Barnard Bee.

g. A cloth sunshade to protect the back of the neck.

Questions 28

a. Which Polish prince became a Marshal of France?

b. Although defeated at Wagram, the Duke of Wellington reckoned him the best of the commanders who fought Napoleon. Who was he?

c. In which US state did the debacle of the Fetterman Massacre (1866) take place?

d. What type of weapon was the Zulu *iklwa*?

e. Who rode a horse known as 'Traveller'?

f. Whose (almost) last words before the Battle of Abu Kru (1885) were, 'First we will have breakfast and then go out to fight.'?

g. What role would the Red Lanterns have performed for Boxers if the units had been given the go-ahead?

Questions 29

a. What role did Frenchman Dupuy de Lome play in the Siege of Paris (1870–71)?

b. Where did Nelson lose his eye?

c. Where in the 1880s did the French face the Chinese-backed Black Flag movement?

d. Which weapon of the 16th and 17th centuries was commonly described as *puissant*?

e. What was the Kentish Knock that gave its name to the battle of that name in 1652?

f. Who said, 'Military science consists in calculating all the chances accurately in the first place and then in giving accident exactly, almost mathematically, its place in one's calculations ... Accident, hazard, chance, call it what you may, a mystery to ordinary minds, becomes a reality to superior men.'?

g. Which action did Sir John Fortescue describe thus, 'It was a battle without a mistake.'?

Questions 30

a. Which one of Napoleon's marshals never lost a battle?

b. Name the commander of the Kimberley garrison during the Second Anglo-Boer War.

c. Of which war was the Battle of the White Mountain the first major engagement?

d. What was the 'Glorious First of June'?

e. Which great French field commander and theorist died of a 'surfeit of women'?

f. Which force did US Grant describe as the most 'efficient army for its number and armament that ever fought a battle'?

g. What name did the Mahdi give to his followers?

Questions 31

a. Who wore a top hat at the Battle of Waterloo, and was killed by a bullet through the temple during a counter-attack?

b. Who reorganised the Prussian General Staff in 1858–59?

c. What did the Battle of Preston in 1715 decide?

d. What was a poll axe?

e. In the American Civil War what was the meaning of the term 'seeing the elephant'?

f. Who wrote to his superiors, "…there has been a hideous confusion as to the number of jars of raspberry jam issued to one cavalry regiment during a sand storm in western Spain. This reprehensive carelessness may be related to the pressure of circumstances since we are at war with France, a fact which may come as a bit of a surprise to you gentlemen in Whitehall.'?

g. After which battle in September 1847 did one Mexican officer say, 'God is a Yankee.'?

Answers 28
a. Poniatowski.
b. Archduke Charles of Austria.
c. Wyoming.
d. A short-hafted thrusting spear with a broad blade.
e. Robert E Lee.
f. General Sir Herbert Stewart.
g. Female auxiliaries providing logistic support in the field.

Answers 29
a. He created a number of armoured trains.
b. Calvi, in the Mediterranean.
c. Annam (Vietnam).
d. The pike.
e. A sandbank in the English Channel – one English vessel, the *Sovereign of the Seas*, ran aground on it during the battle.
f. Napoleon.
g. Sir Harry Smith's victory at Aliwal, First Anglo-Sikh War (1846).

Answers 30
a. Davout: in 1813–14 he successfully defended Hamburg until ordered to surrender by Louis XVIII, the new ruler of France; and in 1815 Napoleon made him Minister of War, so he was not present during the Waterloo campaign.
b. Lieutenant-Colonel Robert Kekewich.
c. The Thirty Years War (1618–48).
d. A sea battle in 1794 in which the Royal Navy, commanded by Admiral Howe, defeated French naval forces.
e. Marshal de Saxe. He had retired to an estate given him by Louis XV after his great successes during the War of Austrian Succession. He had always been a libertine; in November 1750, he 'interviewed' a troupe of eight actresses and died of what his death certificate stated was '*une surfeit de femmes*'.
f. The US Army during the war against Mexico (1846–48).
g. Ansars.

Answers 31
a. Sir Thomas Picton.
b. The Count Helmuth von Moltke (the elder).
c. A Jacobite rising.
d. A short staffed weapon with an axe blade on one side and a hammer head on the other, usually carried by cavalrymen in the 17th century.
e. Seeing combat.
f. Wellington, responding to complaints about his army's bureaucratic records during the Peninsular War.
g. Chapultepec.

Questions 32

a. Which 17th century admiral tied a broom to his masthead to indicate his intention to 'sweep the British from the seas'?

b. Name the commander of the Alamo garrison (1836).

c. At what battle was Cromwell outmanoeuvred by Leslie's Scots, but then won by a daring morning assault?

d. What, during the American Civil War, were 'Pook's Turtles'?

e. How many of Napoleon's marshals did Wellington face in the Peninsula?

f. Who said, '*Nous sommes dans un pot de chambre et nous y serons emmerdés*' ('We are in a chamber pot and we will be shat on') at Sedan (1870)?

g. When was the shako adopted by the British Army?

Questions 33

a. Who completely reorganised French artillery in the two decades before the French Revolution, and therefore laid down one of the foundation stones of Napoleon's method of warfare?

b. Name the Mahdi's successor.

c. At which battle of the American Civil War did the boy-cadets of the Virginia Military Institute make their debut?

d. What, in the early 18th century, was a hanger?

e. Name the Japanese commander at the Battle of Tsushima (1905).

f. Who said, 'Hard pounding this, gentlemen; try who can pound the longest.'?

g. Which Scottish regiment formed the 'thin red line' at Balaklava in 1854?

Questions 34

a. Who was 'Old Fritz'?

b. Which English adventurer was known as the 'White Rajah of Sarawak'?

c. What close connection did American Civil War General William Sherman, born in 1820, have with the Battle of the Fallen Timbers (1811)?

d. Who is known as the 'Father of American naval ordnance'?

e. How did Minister of the Interior Gambetta escape from the capital during the siege of Paris (1870–71)?

f. Who wrote to his mistress, 'I am envious only of glory; for if it be a sin to covet glory, I am the most offending soul alive.'?

g. Who wrote to his wife in late 1860, 'I am strong for the Union, and if things become no worse I hope to continue so.'?

Questions 35

a. Which Confederate general had been vice-president of the United States?

b. Where did the Zulus destroy Henry Pulleine's British forces?

c. Which battle of 1896 saw Abyssinian forces defeat the Italians?

d. What was Napoleon's first victory over the Austrians in Italy in 1796?

e. What was the difference between a matchlock and a flintlock?

f. Who said, 'What ought to be done, I know only too well; what is going to be done, only the gods know.'?

g. What did Czar Alexander II call, 'one of the finest things done in military history'?

Answers 32

a. Dutch Admiral Maarten van Tromp.

b. Lieutenant-Colonel William Travis.

c. Dunbar (1650).

d. A type of ironclad designed by Samuel Pook.

e. Six: Bessieres, Soult, Victor, Jourdan, Masséna, Marmont.

f. French General Ducrot.

g. December 1800, to replace the felt hat.

Answers 33

a. Jean Baptiste de Vaquette Gribeauval.

b. The Khalifa, Abdullah the Taiaishi.

c. Newmarket (1864).

d. A short sword carried by infantry.

e. Admiral Heihachiro Togo.

f. The Duke of Wellington at the Battle of Waterloo.

g. 93rd Highlanders.

Answers 34

a. Frederick the Great – *Der Alte Fritz*.

b. James Brooke.

c. Sherman's middle name was Tecumseh, that of the great Native American commander in the battle.

d. Admiral John Dahlgren.

e. By balloon.

f. Nelson, misquoting from Shakespeare's Henry V, in a letter to Lady Hamilton, 1800.

g. Thomas 'Stonewall' Jackson.

Answers 35

a. General John Breckinridge.

b. Isandhlwana, 1879.

c. Adowa.

d. Montenotte.

e. The former fired by directly applying a lighted match to the pan, whereas in the latter a flint striking steel supplied a spark that ignited the powder.

f. Scharnhorst in 1806, just before the battles of Jena and Auerstadt, commenting on how his advice was ignored by the Prussian commander, the Duke of Brunswick.

g. The capture of Plevna from the Turks (1877).

Questions 36

a. Which of Louis XIV's generals led armies against French forces?

b. Which US ex-Congressman was killed at the Alamo?

c. Who failed to do what at Champigny in 1870?

d. At which battle did Lord Raglan, British commander in the Crimea, lose his right arm?

e. What type of weapon was a native Australian's *nulla nulla*?

f. Which battle of the American Civil War was described by Sherman as 'one of the best-planned battles of the war, but one of the worst-fought'?

g. What item of military clothing was a kittel?

Questions 37

a. Which Royalist general went into exile after Marston Moor, saying, 'I will not endure the laughter of the court.'?

b. Name the second French commander-in-chief during the Crimean War.

c. Which battle saw Shaka Zulu decisively defeat the Ndwandwe in 1818?

d. What happened at Spithead and the Nore in 1797?

e. Who was Robert E Lee describing when he said, 'He fights his troops well and takes good care of them.'?

f. What was 'sleazy'?

g. Who were known as 'Bitter Enders'?

Questions 38

a. Which former Confederate commander died after contracting pneumonia at the funeral of General Sherman?

b. At which battle of the Zulu War did Colonel Redvers Buller win a Victoria Cross?

c. At which English Civil War battle did the Royalist Cornish infantry charge with the battle cry, 'Let us fetch those cannon.'?

d. What were Quaker guns?

e. Which English general of the American War of Independence appears in George Bernard Shaw's play *The Devil's Disciple*?

f. Who said, 'A battle sometimes decides everything; and sometimes the most trifling thing decides the fate of a battle.'?

g. Who said, 'The first duty of a soldier is obedience; the second to fire low.'?

Questions 39

a. On whose behalf did the 'Conway Cabal' operate during the American War of Independence?

b. Whose imprisonment of British subjects led to the Abyssinian Expedition of 1868?

c. What was the War of Devolution?

d. Which American captain dictated peace terms 'at the mouths of cannon' in North Africa in 1815?

e. What additional meaning did the phrase '12 apostles' have during the English Civil War?

f. At which battle of the American-Mexican War is US General Zachary Taylor supposed to have said, 'A little more grape, Captain Bragg.'?

g. The cavalry of which Union State were known as 'Wolverines'?

Answers 36

a. The Prince de Condé. During the Fronde civil war in France his party was worsted and he led Spanish forces against the French in Flanders.

b. David Crockett.

c. The French failed to cut through the Prussian siege lines around Paris.

d. Waterloo.

e. A hardwood throwing club.

f. First Bull Run/Manassas.

g. A type of loose-fitting fatigue tunic.

Answers 37

a. The Earl of Newcastle.

b. General François Canrobert.

c. Gqoki Hill.

d. Naval mutinies.

e. General Ambrose Powell Hill.

f. The neck cloths worn by English 18th century troops were made from inferior material called 'sleazy'.

g. Boer commandos who fought to the end of the Second Anglo-Boer War.

Answers 38

a. General Joseph E Johnston.

b. Hlobane.

c. Lansdown (1643).

d. Fake cannon, usually of wood.

e. General John Burgoyne.

f. Napoleon, in a letter on St Helena.

g. Sir Charles Napier.

Answers 39

a. Horatio Gates – the cabal was a conspiracy attempting to replace Washington with Gates. Conway was an Irish-French soldier prominent in the plotting.

b. King Theodore.

c. A struggle between France on the one hand and Holland, Britain and Sweden on the other (1667–68).

d. Stephen Decatur in the Algerian War.

e. They were the nickname for the 12 wooden flasks containing powder charges on a musketeer's bandolier.

f. Buena Vista.

g. Michigan.

Questions 40

a. Which French revolutionary general was hammered so often that his men nicknamed him 'the anvil'?

b. At which battle is American commander Israel Putnam supposed to have said, 'Don't fire until you see the whites of their eyes.'?

c. Which battle ended the Ashanti War of 1874?

d. Which revolutionary capital ship was launched on 10 February 1906?

e. How was Admiral Nelson's body returned to England after Trafalgar?

f. Who, perhaps surprisingly, said, 'It is admitted by all military men that infantry is the great lever of war, and that artillery and cavalry are only indispensable accessories ...'?

g. Whose dying words were, 'Tell the men to fire faster and not to give up the ship. Fight her till she sinks.'?

Questions 41

a. Name the three emperors present at the Battle of Austerlitz in 1805.

b. What was the Convention of Cintra (1808)?

c. What famous siege did Polish forces raise in 1683?

d. What was an *induna enkula*?

e. Name the world's first ironclad warship.

f. At which battle did Stonewall Jackson exclaim, 'Half an hour, men, only half an hour; can you stand it for half an hour?'?

g. Which English Civil War formation was nicknamed 'Skippon's brave boys'?

Questions 42

a. Who was known as the 'Swamp Fox' during the American War of Independence?

b. From what disability did the Mexican General Santa Anna suffer?

c. At what battle did the 'Ironsides' make their first appearance?

d. What were 'Swedish feathers'?

e. What were the *chatas*, used by the Paraguayan forces in the War of the Triple Alliance (1865–70)?

f. Who remarked, 'As to moral courage, I have rarely met with two o'clock in the morning courage: I mean unprepared courage.'?

g. Which Parliamentarian general said to Cromwell: 'If we beat the king nine and ninety times, yet he is king still ... but if the king beat us once we shall be hanged.'?

Questions 43

a. Who was the defeated French commander at the Heights of Abraham in 1759?

b. Who was the first British commander-in-chief of the Second Anglo-Boer War?

c. At which battle in 1801 did the 28th Foot fight back-to-back, earning the right to wear their famous 'back badge'?

d. What useful addition to the infantryman's equipment did Marshal Vauban invent?

e. What was the claim to fame of the horse 'Comanche'?

f. Who said, '...as I would deserve and keep the kindness of this army, I must let them see that when I expose them, I would not exempt myself.'?

g. What were 'Butler's Rangers' and 'Butler's Legion'?

Answers 40

a. Jourdan – who later became a Napoleonic marshal.

b. Bunker Hill (1775).

c. Kumasi.

d. HMS *Dreadnought.*

e. Pickled in a barrel of brandy.

f. Marshal Ney.

g. Captain James Lawrence of the USS *Chesapeake* during the fight against HMS *Shannon* in 1813.

Answers 41

a. Napoleon I of France, Francis I of Austria and Alexander I of Russia.

b. A controversial agreement between British and French commanders in Portugal, by which the French were allowed to leave the country despite their defeat.

c. The siege of Vienna. John Sobieski, the Polish King, personally led the cavalry charge that broke Turkish resistance.

d. A Zulu field commander.

e. France's *La Gloire* in 1858.

f. Second Manassas/Bull Run (August 1862).

g. The London Trained Bands.

Answers 42

a. US General Francis Marion.

b. He lost a leg repulsing a French attack on Vera Cruz in 1839.

c. Cromwell led a troop of horse at Edgehill in 1642, but the Ironsides really took shape in 1643 when he was authorised to raise a double regiment of horse. On 13 May 1643, this unit distinguished itself at the Battle of Grantham. The first use of the word 'Ironside', however, is usually ascribed to Prince Rupert, commenting on Cromwell's men at Marston Moor (July 1644).

d. Sharpened stakes set in the ground to protect musketeers from cavalry.

e. Oar-powered, flat-bottomed galleys mounting a single heavy cannon.

f. Napoleon, quoted on St. Helena.

g. The Earl of Manchester.

Answers 43

a. Louis Joseph de Montcalm.

b. Sir Redvers Buller.

c. Alexandria.

d. The socket bayonet – a vast improvement on the plug bayonet.

e. It was the only survivor of Custer's command at the Little Big Horn (1876).

f. The Duke of Marlborough.

g. Loyalist units in the American War of Independence. Named after different Butlers, they shared a well-earned reputation for savagery.

Questions 44

a. How did Ulysses S Grant gain his nickname of 'Unconditional Surrender Grant'?
b. In 1774, what was Kutchuk Kainardji and what did it signify?
c. At which battle was Gustavus Adolphus killed?
d. What was 'Nelson's patent bridge for the boarding of first rates'?
e. What was the name of Prince Rupert's dog, killed at Marston Moor?
f. Who said, 'The British soldier can stand up to anything except the British War Office.'?
g. Who said, 'The whole art of war consists of a well-reasoned and extremely circumspect defensive followed by rapid and audacious attack.'?

Questions 45

a Which Calvinist general of the Thirty Years War was known as the 'Attila of Christendom'?
b. At the Battle of Friedland (1807), who was described by a subordinate as appearing 'like the God of war incarnate'?
c. Causeway Heights and Fedioukine Hills. Which battle?
d. What did Captain Whinyate's men fire at Waterloo?
e. The carnage witnessed at which battle led to the creation of the Red Cross?
f. French General Bourbaki remarked, 'We are too old for a war like this', before which battle of the Franco-Prussian War?
g. Who said, 'The bullet is a fool, the bayonet a fine fellow.'?

Questions 46

a. Which Confederate general was known as 'Old Bory'?
b. Which Grand Master of the Teutonic Knights defeated the Russians at the Seritsa River?
c. Name the three British defeats of 'Black Week' during the Second Anglo-Boer War.
d. As a result of what battle was General Gage dismissed as commander-in-chief of British troops in North America?
e. Name Britain's first Secretary of State for War, appointed in 1794.
f. Which master of logistics said, 'An army cannot preserve good order unless its soldiers have meat in their bellies, coats on their backs and shoes on their feet.'?
g. Name the three benefits that would accrue to a winner of the Imperial Russian St George Cross.

Questions 47

a. Who was the inspiring Russian commander who died directing the defence of Sevastopol during the Crimean War?
b. By what name is Mohammed Ahmed Ibu Al-Sayed Abdulah better known?
c. Which battle secured Texan independence from Mexico?
d. Which British admiral commanded the Chilean, Brazilian and Greek navies while under a cloud for being accused of stock exchange fraud?
e. Which Royalist leader had his brains dashed out with his own wooden leg at the siege of Drogheda in 1649?
f. Who said, 'I hold the maxim no less applicable to public than to private affairs, that honesty is the best policy.'?
g. Whose rallying cry was, 'Support the Quing, destroy the foreign devils.'?

Answers 44

a. He demanded and got the unconditional surrender of Confederate Fort Donelson in February 1862.

b. It was a treaty between Catherine the Great's Russia and the Ottoman Empire. The terms were practically dictated by the Russians, and Russian expansion south at Ottoman expense was confirmed as the major aim of Russian foreign policy.

c. Lützen (1632).

d. A popular phrase used to describe his great achievement at the Battle of Cape St Vincent, when he captured one Spanish ship-of-the-line and then boarded another across the deck of the first, thus using the first ship as a bridge to the second.

e. Boy.

f. George Bernard Shaw.

g. Napoleon.

Answers 45

a. Count Ernst von Mansfeld.

b. Marshal Ney, during the attack on the town of Friedland.

c. Balaklava (1854).

d. Rockets.

e. Solferino (1859); the slaughter was witnessed by Henri Dunant, the founder of the Red Cross.

f. Mars-la-Tour (16 August 1870).

g. Russian Marshal Alexander Suvorov.

Answers 46

a. General Pierre Beauregard.

b. Walter von Plettenberg.

c. Colenso, Stormberg and Magersfontein.

d. Bunker Hill (June 1775). He turned over his command to William Howe that October.

e. Henry Dundas.

f. The Duke of Marlborough.

g. Instant promotion, increased pay and exemption from corporal punishment.

Answers 47

a. Admiral Pavel Nakhimov.

b. The Mahdi.

c. San Jacinto (1836).

d. Thomas Cochrane. He was in South America from 1818; and in Greece from 1825–28. He was reinstated in the Royal Navy in 1832.

e. Sir Arthur Aston. His leg had been lost not in action but in an accident while showing off before some ladies on horseback earlier in the decade.

f. George Washington.

g. The Chinese Boxers during the Boxer Rebellion.

Questions 48

a. Name one of the three 'generals at sea' created to lead the English navy in 1649.

b. Who became commander-in-chief of the US Army in 1884?

c. Name Italian General Arimondi's 1893 victory over the Dervishes.

d. What war was known as the 'Potato War'?

e. When were grenadiers first formed?

f. Which Confederate general said, 'I would not give a single man of my command for a fruitless victory.'?

g. What type of troops were Santa Anna's *zapadores*?

Questions 49

a. Suraja Dowlah was defeated by which British commander?

b. Name the two VC winners who died trying to save the Queen's Colours of the 24th Regiment during the Battle of Isandhlwana (1879).

c. Which Turkish defeat led directly to British and French involvement in the Crimean War?

d. Why was the early musket called 'arquebus' or 'hook-gun'?

e. Which English Civil War cavalry commander later invented the mezzotint printing process?

f. Of whom, and on what occasion, did Wellington remark, 'I have you at last.'?

g. What was a powder monkey?

Questions 50

a. Who was 'Black Bob'?

b. Whose fate was sealed at the 'Battle' of Glenrowan Inn (1880)?

c. In which military station did the first widespread unrest of the Indian Mutiny take place?

d. Name the Confederate ironclad forced to surrender at Mobile Bay (1864).

e. Which cavalier is alleged to have said to a parliamentarian firing squad as he beckoned them nearer, 'Friends, I have been nearer to you when you have missed me.'?

f. What general gave the following as the reason for his success, 'I attribute it entirely to the application of good sense to the circumstances of the moment.'?

g. Why was Sir Arthur Haselrig's cavalry regiment of the 1640s called 'lobsters'?

Questions 51

a. Who was Benedict Arnold's English go-between, who, when abandoned, met his death with great dignity?

b. Whose despatches from the Crimea alerted the British public to the Army's lack of preparedness?

c. Name the battle of the Second Afghan War which saw a British column virtually annihilated.

d. What was a spontoon?

e. Japanese Admiral Ito versus Chinese Admiral Ting. Which battle of 1894?

f. Who described himself thus: 'I have not the particular shining bauble or feather in my cap for crowds to gaze or kneel at, but I have power and resolution for forces to tremble at.'?

g. Which war was ended by the Peace of Vereeniging?

Answers 48

a. Robert Blake, Edward Popham, Richard Deane.

b. General Philip Sheridan.

c. Agordat.

d. The war of Bavarian Succession (1778–79) between Austria and Prussia.

e. In 1667, men throwing grenades were introduced into Louis XIV's
Regiment du Roi; then in 1670, 29 French line infantry regiments were ordered
to set up a grenadier company each.

f. General James Longstreet.

g. Assault pioneers/sappers.

Answers 49

a. Robert Clive at Plassey in 1759.

b. Lieutenants Melvill and Coghill.

c. Sinope 1853.

d. Because of the shape of its butt.

e. Prince Rupert, together with Ludwig von Siegen, during the 1650s.

f. Marshal Nicolas-Jean de Dieu Soult, Due de Dalmatie, when he was attending the
coronation of Queen Victoria.

g. A boy who carried powder from the magazine to the guns on an 18th century vessel.

Answers 50

a. Robert Craufurd, commander of the Light Division during the Peninsular War until
his death in 1812 at the siege of Ciudad Rodrigo.

b. Ned Kelly.

c. Meerut, May 1857.

d. The CSS *Tennessee*.

e. Sir George Lisle, 1648.

f. The Duke of Wellington.

g. Because they wore full cuirassier armour.

Answers 51

a. Major John Andre.

b. William Russell, correspondent of *The Times*.

c. Maiwand 1880.

d. A staff weapon, normally about two metres (seven foot) long, carried by officers
in the late 17th/early 18th centuries.

e. Yalu River.

f. Oliver Cromwell.

g. The Second Anglo-Boer War. It was signed in 1902.

Questions 52

a. Who raised the Green Mountain Boys to fight against New York State but was voted out of his command when they fought against the British?

b. When was the Battle of Fontenoy?

c. Which Southern port did Sherman present to Lincoln as 'a Christmas present' in 1864?

d. What technical problem had disastrous results for William III's forces at the Battle of Killiekrankie (1689)?

e. During the English Civil War, who or what was 'Sweet Lips'?

f. Who said, 'It is an ancient rule of war and I am just repeating it – if you separate your forces you will be beaten in detail.'?

g. What type of troops filled the ranks of the French Blue Division during the Franco-Prussian War?

Questions 53

a. Which Napoleonic marshal, nicknamed the 'Iron Marshal', commanded the French right flank at Austerlitz (December 1805)?

b. Who commanded the combined Anglo-Russian force in the Helder Campaign (1799)?

c. At which English Civil War battle was Thomas Fairfax's command almost driven off the field by Goring's Royalist cavalry?

d. What was the name of the Japanese flagship at the Battle of Tsushima (1905)?

e. Who was the original Martinet?

f. Who said, 'Our object ought to be to have a good army rather than a large one.'?

g. What was the difference between Napoleon's Old and Young Guard?

Questions 54

a. Who commanded the British troops at Minden (1759)?

b. Whose hand is revered by the French Foreign Legion?

c. At which battle was JEB Stuart mortally wounded?

d. In the English Civil War, which commander experimented with horse artillery?

e. What is the meaning of the name Chickamauga?

f. Who said to whom: 'Dogs, would you live forever?'?

g. What was the fate of many members of the Mexican Army's San Patricio Battalion during the American-Mexican War?

Questions 55

a. Which two Napoleonic marshals shared the nickname 'the bravest of the brave' (le brave des braves)!

b. Who was the Russian field commander at Balaklava (1854)?

c. Name the fort where Colonel Pearson was besieged during the Zulu War.

d. Name the US victor of the Battle of Manila Bay (1898).

e. Which 16th century Dutch commander is reckoned to have been painted in a portrait more than any other general?

f. Who said, 'The French are what they were in Caesar's time and as he described them, brave to excess but unstable ...'?

g. What was a tuck in the English Civil War?

Answers 52

a. Ethan Allen.

b. 11 May 1745.

c. Savannah.

d. Once they had fitted their plug bayonets they could not fire their muskets, and the Scots rebels took full advantage.

e. A 32-pounder cannon captured by the Royalists at Newark and named after a well-known Hull whore.

f. Frederick the Great.

g. Marines.

Answers 53

a. Davout.

b. The Duke of York.

c. Marston Moor (1644). Cromwell saved the day by swinging his wing round to take Goring's men in the flank.

d. Mikasa.

e. Commander of Louis XIV's Regiment du Roi, whose men were seen to be models of discipline during the campaign of 1667. Martinet died in action in 1672.

f. William of Orange.

g. Eligibility for the Old Guard was five years' service and two campaigns, whereas the Young Guard comprised the best students from each year's conscript class.

Answers 54

a. The Duke of Brunswick.

b. The (false) hand of Captain Danjou, who commanded the Legionnaires of Camerone (1863), has pride of place among the Legion's military relics,

c. Yellow Tavern (May 1865).

d. Prince Rupert, during 1643.

e. River of Blood.

f. Frederick the Great to his Guards, who seemed unwilling to advance at the Battle of Koln (1757).

g. Deserters from the US Army, when captured, many were hanged.

Answers 55

a. Marshals Ney and Lannes.

b. General P Liprandi.

c. Eshowe.

d. Commodore George Dewey.

e. William the Silent, who was a very common subject for Dutch painters of the 16th and 17th centuries.

f. Marshal de Saxe, writing to Frederick the Great in 1746.

g. The sword carried by common infantrymen.

Questions 56

a. Which self-styled 'Napoleon of the West' was also known as the 'Immortal Three-Fourths' and the 'Hero of Tampico'?

b. Who, on witnessing the Charge of the Light Brigade, exclaimed, 'C'est magnifique, mais ce n'est pas la guerre.' ('It is magnificent, but it isn't war.')?

c. At which English Civil War battle did Sir Jacob Ashley offer the prayer, 'Lord, thou knowest how busy I am, or will be, this day; if I forget thee, do not thou forget me. March on, boys.'?

d. Who would be equipped with *Patu Onewa* and *Toki Poto*?

e. What is the meaning of the name Apache?

f. Who said to a captured deserter, 'Come, come, let us fight another battle today: if I am beaten we will desert together tomorrow.'?

g. Who said, 'In war something must be allowed to chance and fortune seeing it is, in its nature, hazardous and an option of difficulties.'?

Questions 57

a. Who was the highest-ranking officer to be killed in the American Civil War?

b. When was Gibraltar first captured by British forces?

c. The Battle of Batoche (1885) ended which rebellion?

d. What type of weapon was manufactured by Chevalier et Grenier, Bollée and Gabert?

e. Who was the real D'Artagnan?

f. Who said, 'The Ancients had a great advantage over us in that their armies were not trailed by a second army of pen-pushers.'?

g. What was the nickname of Rimington's Scouts in the Second Anglo-Boer War?

Questions 58

a. Which 17th century general held to the maxim that 'war should feed war'?

b. Which engineer improved Sevastopol's defences during the Crimean War?

c. Who was the last British monarch to accompany his men into battle?

d. How old was Don John of Austria when he won the Battle of Lepanto (1571)?

e. Who said, 'The whole art of war consists in getting at what lies on the other side of the hill, or, in other words, what we do not know from what we do know.'?

f. Who said, 'The success of my whole project is founded on the firmness of conduct of the officer who will command it.'?

g. Why did the British Army's Colonel Hale adopt the skull and crossbones and motto 'or Glory' for his newly raised regiment of Light Dragoons (later the 17th Lancers) in 1759?

Questions 59

a. Who was 'the bloody butcher'?

b. Who was known as the 'Rock of Chickamauga'?

c. The bloody Taiping Rebellion (1851–65) was also known by what name?

d. What was a saker?

e. Admiral Sir Edward Codrington versus Ibrahim Pasha. Which battle of 1827?

f. Who was Jenkins of the War of Jenkins' Ear (1739–48)?

g. Who said, 'If there is one area where severity is necessary for a sovereign, it is with regard to his soldiers.'?

Answers 56

a. Mexican President-General Antonio de Lopez Santa Anna.

b. French General Bosquet.

c. Edgehill (1642).

d. Maoris. They are a type of club and long-shafted tomahawk.

e. It is derived from a word meaning enemy.

f. Frederick the Great.

g. James Wolfe, in a letter of November 1757.

Answers 57

a. Confederate General Albert Sidney Johnston, commander of the Army of Mississippi, killed at Shiloh (April 1862).

b. In 1704, during the War of Spanish Succession. The acquisition was formalised in 1713 at the Treaty of Utrecht.

c. Louis Riel's Metis uprising in present-day Manitoba.

d. The Mitrailleuse (early French machine gun).

e. Captain of the 1st Company of Louis XIV's *Mousquetaires de la Garde* from 1667 until his death at the siege of Maastricht in 1673.

f. Napoleon.

g. 'Tigers', because of the wild-cat skin worn around their headgear.

Answers 58

a. Wallenstein.

b. Colonel Todleben.

c. George II at Dettingen, 1743.

d. 23. He owed his command first to his status as a bastard son of the Emperor Charles V and half-brother of Philip II of Spain, and secondly to his successful campaign against the Spanish Moriscos (1569–70).

e. The Duke of Wellington.

f. Frederick the Great, *Instruction to his Generals*.

g. In memory of his friend and comrade-in-arms, General James Wolfe, killed at Quebec in the same year.

Answers 59

a. The Duke of Cumberland, so nicknamed because of his activities after the Battle of Culloden (1746).

b. Union General George Thomas.

c. The War of Heavenly Peace.

d. A light cannon used in the English Civil War.

e. Navarino.

f. Captain Jenkins, a merchant captain whose ear was allegedly cut off by Spanish forces that captured his vessel in the Caribbean. This incident sparked off popular fury in England and forced Prime Minister Walpole, unwillingly, to go to war with Spain in 1739.

g. Louis XIV.

Questions 60
a. Who surrendered at Ulm (October 1805)?
b. What was Bengali Sipahi Mangal Pande's claim to fame?
c. Which treaty brought an end to the Thirty Years War?
d. Laing's Nek, Ingogo, Double Drift. Which war?
e. Who was responsible for overseeing the expansion of the Union's railroad network in the American Civil War?
f. Who said, 'It is evident that up to now a taste for plunder has been one of the principal attractions that has caused many to choose the soldier's trade.'?
g. Who said, 'The art of war consists in bringing to bear with an inferior army a superiority of force at the point at which one attacks or is attacked.'?

Questions 61
a. Whose *Essai générale de tactique* of 1772, advocating a citizen's army and a war of manoeuvre, was described by Napoleon as 'a book suitable for shaping great men.'?
b. Name the Turkish commander-in-chief in the Crimea.
c. What was the final battle of Stonewall Jackson's 1862 Valley Campaign?
d. When did red coats become standard for the British army?
e. Which great French admiral (and successful privateer) entered the Dutch navy as a youth?
f. Who said, 'When we assumed the soldier we did not lay aside the citizen.'?
g. Who did Simon Bolivar describe as the '*Salvadores de me Patria*'?

Questions 62
a. Who commanded the French forces at the disaster of Rossbach in 1757?
b. Name the leader of the 1870 insurrection in Canada against the Act of Confederation.
c. Which German town was plundered and razed to the ground by the imperialist General Tilly in May 1631 in what was probably the single worst atrocity of the Thirty Years War?
d. What in the American Civil War were 'Davids'?
e. Where was Florence Nightingale's hospital during the Crimean War?
f. Who said, 'In battle, most men expose themselves enough to satisfy the needs of honour; few wish to do more than this ...'?
g. Who said, 'Popularity, however desirable it may be to individuals, will not form, or feed, or pay an army; will not enable it to march and fight; will not keep it in a state of efficiency for long and arduous service.'?

Questions 63
a. Which leading French general, and one-time rival of Napoleon, was killed by a cannon ball at the Battle of Dresden (1813) while advising the Allies?
b. Who commanded the British Heavy Brigade at the Battle of Balaklava (1854)?
c. Name the major Jacobite success during the '45.
d. Chapultepec, Churubusco, Cerro Gordo. Which war?
e. What was a zariba?
f. Who described his first battle thus: 'I know that my heart was pounding when reveille sounded on the morning of that fateful day.'?
g. Who were the Whitecoats or the Lambs in 1644?

Answers 60
a. The Austrian General Mack.
b. A corruption of his name – 'Pandies' – was used to describe Indian mutineers by British troops, 1857–58.
c. The Treaty of Westphalia (1648).
d. The First Anglo-Boer War (1881).
e. General Herman Haupt.
f. Louis XIV.
g. Napoleon.

Answers 61
a. The Comte de Guibert.
b. Omar Pasha.
c. Port Republic, 8 June.
d. 1645, with the New Model Army.
e. Jean Bart, who served under De Ruyter until he returned to French service in 1672.
f. George Washington, addressing the provincial congress of New York in 1775.
g. The troops of his British Legion.

Answers 62
a. The marquis de Soubise.
b. Louis Riel.
c. Magdeburg.
d. Low-freeboard, steam-powered torpedo boats.
e. Scutari, Turkey.
f. Francois de la Rochefoucauld, *Refléxions ou sentences et maximes morales*, written in 1665.
g. The Duke of Wellington, in a letter of April 1811.

Answers 63
a. Moreau.
b. General James Scarlett.
c. Prestonpans (September 1745).
d. The American-Mexican War (1845–48).
e. A temporary defensive position, usually made of thorn bushes.
f. Frederick the Great. He was describing the battle of Mollwitz (April 1741).
g. The Duke of Newcastle's regiment.

Questions 64

a. Whose first great victory was at Breitenfeld?

b. Who led the relief column that finally relieved Lucknow during the Indian Mutiny?

c. What province of the Austrian Empire did Frederick the Great invade in 1740?

d. What breach-loading rifle was used by the French during the Franco-Prussian War (1870–71)?

e. After what battle did the military band of the defeated army play *The World Turned Upside Down*?

f. Who said, 'No-one can answer for his courage when he has never been in danger.'?

g. How did the Zulus 'solve one of the most difficult problems of French history' in 1879?

Questions 65

a. Who commanded the French troops at the Battle of Valmy (1792)?

b. What was the profession of Confederate General Leonidas Polk?

c. Which English regiment was wiped out retreating from Kabul to Jalalabad in 1842?

d. Who was the Royal Navy commander at the Battle of Lagos Bay, Portugal (1759)?

e. Who were 'third class devils' to the Chinese Boxers?

f. In what unit was the anonymous infantryman who wrote: 'I looked amongst the line; it was enough to reassure me. The steady determined scowl of my companions assured my heart and gave me determination.'?

g. What was the name of the French irregulars who fought in the Franco-Prussian War?

Questions 66

a. Who was defeated at Poltava (1709)?

b. Name the Union Army's four commanders-in-chief during the Civil War.

c. How many VCs were awarded for the defence of Rorke's Drift?

d. What was a carronade?

e. Name the commander of the Imperial Russian fleet at Tsushima (1905).

f. Who said, 'A cavalry general should be a master of practical science, know the value of seconds, despise life and not trust to chance.'?

g. In the 17th century, what type of soldier wore a morion?

Questions 67

a. Which English Civil War general was nicknamed 'William the Conqueror'?

b. Who commanded the British forces during the Zulu War?

c. Where would you have found Flagstaff Tower, Ludlow Castle and Metcalfe House?

d. Name the two ironclads that clashed at Hampton Roads in 1862.

e. What was the origin of the expression a 'forlorn hope'?

f. Who said: 'Decline the attack unless you can make it with advantage.'?

g. Who said: 'A soldier will fight long and hard for a bit of coloured ribbon.'?

Answers 64
a. Gustavus Adolphus, 1631.
b. General Sir Colin Campbell.
c. Silesia. The War of Austrian Succession is sometimes known as the Silesian Wars,
d. The *chassepot.*
e. Yorktown (1781).
f. Duke de la Rochefoucauld, *Refléxions ou sentences et maximes morales.*
g. By killing Louis, Prince Imperial of France, only son of Emperor Napoleon III, thereby ensuring the continuation of a republic.

Answers 65
a. Dumouriez.
b. Bishop of the Episcopalian Church.
c. The 44th Foot.
d. Edward Boscawen, 'Old Dreadnought'. He captured three and sank two of the twelve-strong French fleet.
e. Chinese who worked for foreigners.
f. The writer was in the British 71st Foot at the Battle of Vimeiro (1808).
g. Francs-Tireurs.

Answers 66
a. Charles XII of Sweden.
b. Scott, McClellan, Halleck and Grant.
c. Eleven.
d. A large-bore small cannon used in warships.
e. Admiral Rozhdestvensky.
f. Napoleon, *Military Maxim 86.*
g. A pikeman; the morion (a helmet with a brim and wide comb) was Spanish in origin but had spread to most European armies by then.

Answers 67
a. William Waller.
b. Lord Chelmsford.
c. Outside Delhi during the Indian Mutiny.
d. The Union *Monitor* and the Confederate *Merrimac.*
e. A thin screen of musketeers placed in front of an army drawn up for battle.
f. Marshal de Saxe, *My Reveries*, 1732.
g. Napoleon, to the captain of HMS *Bellepheron*, taking him to exile in 1815.

Questions 68

a. 'Old Rosy' was the nickname of which American Civil War general?

b. Which side had the most men at the Battle of Naseby?

c. Which battle was fought in Egypt on 13 September 1882?

d. What were languets?

e. What act of bravery did Brigadier Row perform at Blenheim?

f. Who said: 'My first wish would be that my Military family, and the whole Army, should consider themselves as a band of brothers, willing and ready to die for each other.'?

g. What was the lobster pot?

Questions 69

a. Which of Napoleon's marshals became King of Sweden?

b. Who was known as the 'Napoleon of the (Native American) Indians'?

c. By what name is the American Civil War Battle of Elkhorn Tavern (March 1862) also known?

d. When did the pike effectively go out of service?

e. Who commanded the British fleet at the Battle of Quiberon Bay (1759)?

f. Who said: 'He supposes all men to be brave at all times and does not realise that the courage of the troops must be reborn daily, that nothing is so variable, and that the true skill of the general consists in knowing how to guarantee it by his dispositions, his positions, and those traits of genius that characterise the great captains.'?

g. Who said: 'Desperate affairs require desperate measures.'?

Questions 70

a. Which 17th century European general was famous for having a personal sorcerer?

b. Who commanded the Army of the Vosges during the Franco-Prussian War?

c. At which battle of 1644 did the victors throw stones before they charged?

d. Name the Confederate commerce raider captained by Raphael Semmes.

e What is the meaning of Mahdi?

f. Who said: 'In half and hour you will see how we shall lose a one (a battle).'?

g. Who said: 'If you wish to be loved by your soldiers, husband their blood and do not lead them to slaughter.'?

Questions 71

a. Who was 'the Old Dessauer'?

b. Which Confederate general's horse was called 'Jeff Davis'?

c. Name the battle that effectively ended the Zulu War in 1879.

d. What weapon was a Maori's *tupara*?

e. Where did de Ruyter's Dutch fleet raid in 1667?

f. Who said, 'I had rather have a plain russet-coated captain that knows what he fights for, and loves what he knows, than that which you call a gentleman and is nothing more.'?

g. What were *voyageurs*?

Answers 68

a. Union General William Rosecrans.

b. The Parliamentarians. They had 13,500 men to the Royalists' 7,500.

c. Tel-el-Kebir.

d. Metal strips holding the head of a pike to the shaft and preventing it being chopped off by cavalrymen,

e. Row led the attack on Blenheim village during the great battle in 1704, and refused to let his men fire until he had thrust his sword into the French palisades. He was killed as he did so.

f. George Washington, in a letter written in 1798.

g. The helmet worn by Cromwell's troopers.

Answers 69

a. Bernadotte, who ruled as Carl XIV (1818–44).

b. Chief Joseph of the Nez Perce.

c. Pea Ridge.

d. In the 1690s, when the socket bayonet enabled a musketeer to protect himself against cavalry. The last units in the French army to carry pikes were Swiss regiments (in French pay), which lost them in 1703.

e. Admiral Edward Hawke.

f. Marshal de Saxe, *My Reveries*.

g. Nelson.

Answers 70

a. Wallenstein.

b. Garibaldi.

c. Tippermuir. Montrose's forces had no firearms, and so he told his men to pick up stones and to use them instead.

d. CSS *Alabama*.

e. The Expected One.

f. The Duke of Conde in response to the Duke of Gloucester's comment that he had never seen a battle just before the Battle of the Dunes (1658).

g. Frederick the Great, *Instructions to his Generals*, 1747.

Answers 71

a. Prince Louis of Annhalt-Dessau, whose genius for training was instrumental in creating the army of Frederick the Great.

b. General John Bell Hood.

c. Ulundi.

d. A double-barrelled shotgun.

e. The Medway estuary, where they burned the dockyard at Chatham.

f. Oliver Cromwell, in a letter of 1643.

g. Canadian boatmen employed to ferry British troops up the Nile (1884).

Questions 72

a. Name the British commander killed at the Battle of Majuba Hill (1881).
b. Who was the youngest officer to attain army command during the American Civil War?
c. Which document brought Scotland into the English Civil War on the side of Parliament, in 1644?
d. Name the first major engagement of the Franco-Prussian War.
e. What, during the Second Anglo-Boer War, were Long Toms?
f. Who said: 'It is an invariable axiom of war to secure your own flanks and rear and endeavour to turn those of the enemy.'?
g. Who said: 'Discipline is the soul of an army. It makes small numbers formidable; procures success to the weak and esteem to all.'?

Questions 73

a. Which 19th century general was known as 'The Liberator'?
b. Which Irish woman was dubbed the 'Heroine of Tampico' for her spying activities during the American-Mexican War?
c. Who laid siege to Detroit in 1763?
d. The sinking of which US Navy capital ship sparked off the Spanish-American War of 1898–99?
e. Where did the word 'infantry' originate?
f. During the English Civil War, who described herself as 'she-majesty, generalissima'?
g. Why would a British officer have worn a gorget during the Peninsular War?

Questions 74

a. Who was the last of Napoleon's marshals to receive his baton?
b. What was Union General George Meade's nickname?
c. What were the four major field actions of the Crimean War?
d. What was a galleass?
e. Who said: 'I will not send troops to danger which I will not myself encounter.'?
f. Who said: '... nothing is sure in a sea fight above all.'?
g. Which force was divided into Rubs?

Questions 75

a. Name the Duke of Wellington's successor as the British Army's commander-in-chief.
b. Name the Union officer in command of Fort Sumter in 1861.
c. Which of his victories did Cromwell describe as being 'a crowning mercy'?
d. Which French admiral conducted a successful campaign against the Royal Navy in the Indian Ocean in the 1780s?
e. By what name were Hondendowah tribesmen better known to British soldiers?
f. Of whom did the Prince of Annhalt-Dessau write, 'The ascendancy of that man is inconceivable. I was unable to utter an angry word; he totally disarmed me in an instant.'?
g. What role did the *Intendance* perform in the French Army of the second half of the 19th century?

Answers 72

a. Sir George Colley.

b. Confederate John Bell Hood, age 33.

c. The Solemn League and Covenant.

d. Wissembourg (4 Augusr 1870).

e. Long-range Boer artillery manufactured by France's Creusot firm.

f. Frederick the Great, *Instructions to his Generals*, 1747.

g. George Washington.

Answers 73

a. Simon Bolivar.

b. Ann Chase.

c. Ottawa chief Pontiac during Pontiac's War.

d. USS *Maine*, in Havana harbour.

e. The Spanish *tercios* of the 16th century were often named after Spanish princes or princesses (the Spanish for princess is *infanta*). Gradually, the *tercios* became known as *infanterios*, hence 'infantry'.

f. Queen Henrietta Maria.

g. Originally an armoured throat guard, by the Napoleonic Wars it had become purely decorative, denoting officer rank.

Answers 74

a. Emmanuel Grouchy, on 15 April 1815. He was Napoleon's 26th marshal.

b. 'Old Snapping Turtle'.

c. Alma, Inkerman, Balaklava and Tchernaya.

d. A large, well-armed galley powered by sails as well as oars.

e. The Duke of Marlborough.

f. Nelson in a memorandum to his fleet in October 1805, just before Trafalgar.

g. The Dervish Army; they were battalions.

Answers 75

a. Lord Hardinge.

b. Major Robert Anderson.

c. Worcester, 1651.

d. Pierre André de Suffren, widely regarded as the outstanding French admiral of the 18th century.

e. 'Fuzzy-Wuzzies'.

f. The Prince was describing how he tried to complain to the Duke of Marlborough about an order he had been given.

g. Field supply and running military hospitals and prisons.

Questions 76

a. Which of Napoleon's marshals was nicknamed 'The Emperor's Wife'?

b. Name the rival commanders at First Bull Run/Manassas.

c. On which hill was the Battle of Bunker Hill fought (1775)?

d. What contribution did Matthew Fontaine Mauny make to the Union's war effort?

e. Who were the wild geese?

f. Who said, 'I would lay down my life for America but I cannot trifle with my honour.!

g. What role did Tigermen play in the Imperial Chinese Army?

Questions 77

a. Where did the Grand Old Duke of York allegedly march his men up and down the hill?

b. What was the importance of Claude Minié?

c. Which town, besieged by the Royalists in 1643, was described as 'a city assailed by man but saved by God'?

d. What was unusual about the timing of the Battle of New Orleans (1815)?

e. Name the captain of the CSS *Merrimac*.

f. Who said, 'In war there is but one favourable moment; the great art is to seize it.'?

g. Who were the 'Shorncliffe Boys'?

Questions 78

a. Name the leader of the diggers at the Eureka Stockade in 1854.

b. What was the nickname of Union General Henry Halleck?

c. At which battle did the Marquis of Granby go at the enemy 'bald-headed'?

d. Why was Villeneuve unlucky in having to fight the Battle of Trafalgar?

e. What was a *spahi*?

f. Who said, 'War must be carried on systematically, and to do that you must have men of character activated by principles of honour.'?

g. In 1809, what was the 'Black Horde'?

Questions 79

a. Who was Pugachev?

b. Which battle freed Bolivia from Spanish control?

c. Gingindlovu, Nyezane and Ntombe. Which war?

d. Attacking across the Pratzen Heights at Austerlitz in 1805, what were Marshal Soult's French infantrymen given to stiffen their resolve?

e. Name the only Northern cavalry unit to carry lances during the American Civil War.

f. Which English Civil War general's prescription for military success was, 'Pay well, command well, hang well.'?

g. Who said: 'My character and good name are in my own keeping. Life with disgrace is dreadful. A glorious death is to be envied.'?

Answers 76

a. His chief of staff, Berthier.

b. Union General Irvin McDowell and Confederate General Pierre Beauregard.

c. Breed's Hill, oddly enough.

d. He was in charge of developing naval torpedoes (mines).

e. Irish mercenaries, who served on the continent of Europe, especially after the accession of William III to the throne.

f. John Paul Jones,

g. They acted as skirmishers

Answers 77

a. Flanders, 1793–95 (although some sources say The Helder 1799).

b. His hollow-based, conoidal lead bullet made rifling practical for muzzle loaders, and greatly increased the destructive nature of infantry fire.

c. Gloucester.

d. It was fought after the Treaty of Ghent which ended the Anglo-American War of 1812–15.

e. Franklin Buchanan.

f. Napoleon, *Military Maxim 95*.

g. The light infantry trained by Sir John Moore at Shorncliffe camp from 1803 to 1806.

Answers 78

a. Peter Lalor of the Miners' Reform League.

b. 'Old Brains'.

c. Warburg (1760).

d. Because Napoleon had already decided that it was impossible to invade England, and had left Boulogne to set out for central Germany with his *Grande Armée*.

e. A Turkish cavalryman of the early modern period.

f. George Washington.

g. A Brunswick corps raised to fight Napoleon under the Duke of Brunswick (who was himself known as 'the Black Duke').

Answers 79

a. A Cossack who sparked off a large-scale revolt of serfs in late-18th century Russia. The rising was put down with great brutality.

b. Tumusla (1825).

c. The Zulu War of 1879.

d. A triple grog ration.

e. The 6th Pennsylvania Regiment (Rush's Lancers).

f. Sir Ralph Hopton, *Maxims for the Management of an Army*.

g. Nelson, in March 1795.

Questions 80
a. Which Confederate commander was described as a 'hard case'?
b. Rodney versus de Grasse: which battle in 1783?
c. About which 'X' was Lord Galway reporting back from Spain in 1704: 'Good X are so scarce, that one must bear with their humours and forgive them, for we cannot be without them.'?
d. What role did the Udibi perform in a Zulu field force?
e. Over which 'battlefield' did the Southern Cross flag fly?
f. Who said, 'Appreciate all those details; they are not without glory. It is the first step that leads to glory.'?
g. Whose dying words were, 'Strike the tent.'?

Questions 81
a. Who were Nelson's 'band of brothers'?
b. Name the victorious US commander at the Battle of Santiago Bay (July 1898).
c. Where did the 'whiff of grapeshot' take place?
d. Name the hard-fighting Confederate unit commanded by Colonel Wheat.
e. What did NNC stand for in the Zulu War?
f. Who said, and on what occasion, 'I have not yet begun to fight.'?
g. Who said, 'Artillery decides everything, and infantry no longer do battle with naked steel.'?

Questions 82
a. Why were the Coldstream Guards so called?
b. Name the massacre allegedly perpetrated by members of Confederate Nathan Bedford Forrest's command in April 1864.
c. Who, at which battle, said, 'Damn the torpedoes.'?
d. Who were known to the Maoris as *pakeha*?
e. Who or what was 'Brown Bess'?
f. Name the two regular English cavalry regiments to serve in the Zulu War.
g. Who said, 'Military art is the art of separating for life and uniting for battle.'?

Questions 83
a. Which American hero of the Battle of Saratoga (1777) later died in penniless obscurity in London?
b. Who was the 'organiser of victory'?
c. Which battle saw over 100,000 Americans on the field for the first time?
d. Which British admiral was shot 'to encourage the others'?
e. On which battlefield of the Franco-Prussian War can be found the museum known as La Maison de la Derniere Cartouche?
f. Who said, 'Put your trust in God and keep your powder dry.'?
g. What was the source of the metal originally used to make the Victoria Cross, Britain's highest award for gallantry?

Answers 80

a. General Braxton Bragg.

b. The Saints, a British naval victory.

c. Engineers.

d. Young boys, they acted as scouts and carried field supplies.

e. The Eureka Stockade, Australia, 1854.

f. Frederick the Great.

g. Confederate General Robert E Lee.

Answers 81

a. His captains in the Mediterranean, during the period leading up to the Battle of the Nile.

b. Commodore Winfield Scott Schley,

c. In Paris, 5 October 1795.

d. The Louisiana Tiger Zouaves.

e. Natal Native Contingent.

f. US Captain John Paul Jones when called upon to surrender by the captain of the Royal Navy vessel *Serapis* (1779).

g. Frederick the Great.

Answers 82

a. Because they marched from Coldstream, on the border between England and Scotland, to London in 1660 to help restore the king.

b. Fort Pillow.

c. Union Admiral David Farragut at the Battle of Mobile Bay (August 1864).

d. White men.

e. The standard musket of the British Army, so nicknamed from the early 18th century until its replacement in 1830.

f. The 1st King's Dragoon Guards and 17th Lancers.

g. Napoleon.

Answers 83

a. Benedict Arnold.

b. Napoleon.

c. Shiloh (April 1862).

d. Admiral Sir John Byng, after an inconclusive action off Minorca in 1756. The quote is from Voltaire's *Candide*.

e. Sedan.

f. Oliver Cromwell.

g. Russian artillery captured during the Crimean War.

From 1914

Questions 1

a. Where did 'the Tiger' beat 'the Rabbit'?

b. Which two countries fought the 'Soccer War'?

c. In which conflict did the first helicopter assault from the sea take place?

d. What did the Butt Report of August 1941 prove?

e. According to British Army legend, what is 'the most dangerous thing in the world'?

f. Where did the multi-national 'Dunsterforce' serve at the end of World War I?

g. Which medal was known to its recipients as the 'Order of the Frozen Meat'?

Questions 2

a. Which British naval officer commanded a squadron of armoured cars in Russian Galicia during the War of Intervention of 1917–19?

b. Name the communications route that ran between Port Moresby and Buna in New Guinea in World War II.

c. What was a 'Big Wing'?

d. What kind of warship is the *Kiev*?.

e. What was renounced by countries signing the Briand-Kellogg Pact of 1927?

f. Who described the Argentine invasion of the Falklands as, 'a most ungentlemanly act'?

g. Which famous child care specialist was prominent in the anti-Vietnam War movement?

Questions 3

a. Who was the first British Secretary of State for Defence?

b. How many Indo-Pakistan Wars have been fought since the partition of 1947?

c. What did the Soviets dub the 'Circle of Death'?

d. In World War I, how was the German Staaken R-VI aircraft better known?

e. Which two Latin American countries contributed forces to Allied operations in World War II?

f. Who said, in 1944, 'The real trouble with the Yanks is that they are completely ignorant as to the rules of the game we are playing with the Germans. You play so much better when you know the rules.'?

g. In which war did the Commonwealth Division fight?

Answers 1
a. Malaya, 1941–42: the Japanese commander, Yamashita, was known as 'the Tiger'; his opponent, Percival, was nicknamed 'the Rabbit'.
b. Honduras and El Salvador.
c. The Anglo-French landings at Suez in 1956.
d. The inaccuracy of the RAF night-precision campaign against German targets; only a third of the bombs were being dropped within five miles of the aiming-point.
e. An officer with a map.
f. At Baku in Azerbaijan under Brigadier-General Lionel Dunsterville.
g. The campaign medal awarded to all German soldiers who were on the Eastern Front during the winter of 1941–42.

Answers 2
a. Lieutenant-Commander Oliver Locker-Lampson.
b. The Kokoda Trail.
c. A grouping of squadrons of fighters during the Battle of Britain to meet German attacks en masse; it proved less flexible than the normal commitment of individual squadrons as they became available.
d. An aircraft carrier.
e. War (except in self-defence). Altogether 65 countries, including Germany, signed.
f. The British Governor, Rex Hunt.
g. Dr Benjamin Spock.

Answers 3
a. Duncan Sandys.
b. Two (1965 and 1971).
c. The use of squadrons of fighter-bombers (usually llyushin Il-2 *Sturmoviks*) to fix and attack German armoured columns in continuous waves.
d. The Riesen or 'Giant' (it had a crew of up to nine),
e. Mexico and Brazil.
f. General Sir Bernard Montgomery.
g. The Korean War.

Questions 4

a. Why was the Canadian Gerald Bull, mysteriously killed in March 1990, important to the Gulf War?

b. In which war did the Battle of Wal Wal (or Ualual) take place?

c. Which US aircraft of World War II was known as the 'Black Widow'?

d What was the Argentine flagship in the Falklands War?

e. Name the Republican candidate for the US Presidency, defeated by Franklin D Roosevelt in November 1944.

f. Whose response to the first atomic test explosion was to remember the Hindu quote: 'I am become death, the destroyer of worlds.'?

g. With which British division did a South African brigade serve on the Western Front in World War I?

Questions 5

a. Which boy sailor won a posthumous Victoria Cross at the Battle of Jutland (1916)?

b. What was the 'Hammelburg Breakout' in March 1945?

c. In the Gulf War, what were MREs?

d. What was unusual about Captain Chuck DeBellevue, the highest scoring ace of the Vietnam War?

e. What rank was reached by Adolf Hitler in World War I?

f. Who was described, at his funeral in 1953, as the 'last great Prussian'?

g. Which British regiment's cap badge shows a World War I tank?

Questions 6

a. Who commanded the British 79th Armoured Division of 'Funnies' in North-West Europe, 1944–45?

b. What name did the Israelis give to their invasion of Lebanon in 1982?

c. What was the F4U better known as?

d. Where in September 1931 did a serious mutiny take place in the Royal Navy?

e. Which Swiss town was inadvertently bombed by US aircraft on 1 April 1944?

f. Who drew 'a line in the sand'?

g. Which island off the coast of Scotland was used during World War II for anthrax experiments?

Questions 7

a. Name the only US serviceman to be shot for desertion in World War II.

b. During the Falklands War, what was Operation Paraquat?

c. What was the Panzerkampfwagen V better known as?

d. Which British admiral, killed at the Battle of Jutland (1916), gave his name to a World War II battleship?

e. Which member of NATO has no armed forces?

f. Which German Combat Badge, instituted in April 1941, featured a Viking ship?

g. Which British infantry division lost the bulk of its men at St Valery-en-Caux on 12 June 1940?

Answers 4

a. He designed The Iraqi 'supergun' and other military pieces.
b. The Italian-Ethiopian War (1935–36).
c. The Northrop P61 night-fighter.
d. 25 de Mayo.
e. Thomas E Dewey.
f. J Robert Oppenheimer.
g. 9th Scottish Division.

Answers 5

a. Boy (1st Class) John Travers Cornwell of HMS *Chester*.
b. A controversial operation ordered by Patton that involved an armoured force penetrating deep behind German lines to release Allied PoWs, who included Patton's son-in-law.
c. Meals Ready to Eat, the American combat ration (often corrupted to 'Meals Rejected by Ethiopians').
d. He was a rear-seat flier, scoring four kills with one pilot and two with another.
e. *Gefreite* or Corporal.
f. Field Marshal Gerd von Rundstedt.
g. The Royal Tank Regiment.

Answers 6

a. Major-General Sir Percy Hobart.
b. Operation Peace for Galilee.
c. The US Navy's Vought Corsair carrier fighter.
d. At Invergordon, among ships of the Atlantic Fleet.
e. Schaffhausen.
f. President George Bush on the despatch of American troops to the Gulf in 1990.
g. Gruinard.

Answers 7

a. Private Eddie Slovik.
b. The British recapture of South Georgia.
c. The Panther tank.
d. Rear-Admiral the Honourable H L A Hood.
e. Iceland.
f. That awarded to crew-members of 'Auxiliary Cruisers' (armed merchant raiders).
g. The 51st (Highland), two brigades of which surrendered.

Questions 8

a. Which Australian major won a posthumous Victoria Cross in the Vietnam War?

b. What was the codename for the Washington conference of Anglo-US planners, held in December 1941 – January 1942?

c. What was meant in World War II by 'blowtorch and corkscrew' fighting?

d. What contribution did French pilot Roland Garros make to air combat in World War I?

e. Who was 'Monty's Double'?

f. Who said he would rather drink poison than make peace – but did it anyway?

g. Who was 'Lord Haw Haw'?

Questions 9

a. Who led the Malayan Resistance to Japanese rule in World War II?

b. Which disastrous defeat by the Viet Minh in 1954 marked the end of French rule in Indochina?

c. What was a *kubelwagen*?

d. Which other German warship accompanied the *Goeben* on her voyage through the Mediterranean to Turkey in August 1914?

e. Of which aircraft is the Xian J-7 a Chinese copy?

f. Who said, and in which battle: 'Come on you sons of bitches, do you want to live forever?'?

g. Which British division in World War II wore a panda's head as its arm badge?

Questions 10

a. Which American journalist first popularised the exploits of Colonel T E Lawrence 'of Arabia' in World War I?

b. What, in the Korean War, was Operation Chromite?

c. What sort of vehicle was a *Schutzenpanzerwagen SdKfz 251*?

d. What was the name of the tanker that, badly damaged, limped into Malta on 15 August 1942?

e. British General Edmund Ironside is alleged to have been the inspiration for which fictional character created by John Buchan?

f. In the Gulf War, what improvised badge was worn by British logistics troops?

g. What did the US Navy acronym WAVES stand for in World War II?

Questions 11

a. Who commanded the German Sixth Panzer Army in the Ardennes, December 1944?

b. What was 'Sickleforce'?

c. Which modern aircraft is known as the 'Warthog'?

d. What was unusual about the French Army's Lafayette Escadrille in 1914–17?

e. What would a German soldier expect a *hiwi* to do?

f. Who wrote, 'The battlefield is cold. It is the lonesomest place which men may share together.'?

g. What were the 'Winter Soldier Hearings'?

Answers 8

a. Major Peter Badcoe in 1967.

b. Arcadia.

c. Blasting the entrance to a Japanese-defended bunker with a flamethrower, then sealing it with a satchel of high explosives; used principally on Okinawa in 1945.

d. He invented a simple device to allow machine guns to fire through an aircraft propeller.

e. The actor Clifford James; he impersonated General Sir Bernard Montgomery and visited Gibraltar in early 1944 in an effort to fool German intelligence about Allied intentions.

f. Ayatollah Khomeini at the end of the Iran-Iraq War in 1988.

g. William Joyce; an American by birth, he broadcast German propaganda to Britain during World War II.

Answers 9

a. Chin Peng (OBE).

b. The siege of Dien Bien Phu.

c. A German cross-country general purpose vehicle, equivalent to the Allies' Jeep.

d. The light cruiser *Breslau*.

e. The Mikoyan MiG-21.

f. Gunnery Sergeant Dan Daly of the US Marine Corps, at Belleau Wood on 6 June 1918.

g. 9th Armoured.

Answers 10

a. Lowell Thomas.

b. The amphibious landing at Inchon in September 1950.

c. A German half-track troop carrier.

d. *Ohio*.

e. Richard Hannay.

f. A Black Adder (from the television series).

g. Women Accepted for Volunteer Emergency Service.

Answers 11

a. General Josef ('Sepp') Dietrich.

b. A British force landed at Aandalsnes (Norway) in April 1940.

c. The Fairchild Republic A-10.

d. It was composed of American volunteer aviators.

e. Fairly mundane tasks; it was the name given to Russian volunteers who worked for German forces on the Eastern Front (from *Hilfswilliger* or Volunteer Auxiliary).

f. Brigadier-General S L A Marshall in his book *Men Against Fire*, based on his observations of battle in World War II.

g. Investigations of American atrocities submitted to Congress in 1970 by Vietnam veterans opposed to the war.

Questions 12
a. Who commanded the French forces in the Gulf War?
b. In which undeclared war in 1939 did General G K Zhukov command the forces of the Soviet Union against the Japanese?
c. Which American heavy tank was first tested in combat in North-West Europe in early 1945?
d. Which warship saw action as a bombardment vessel in both the Korean War and the Gulf War?
e. Which aircraft were nicknamed 'Faith', 'Hope', and 'Charity'?
f. Who said, just before committing suicide in April 1945, 'I would never have thought that I would ever be so disappointed. My only aim was to serve Germany.'?
g. What in World War I was a funk jacket?

Questions 13
a. Who was commanding the US Pacific Fleet at the time of the Japanese attack on Pearl Harbor in December 1941?
b. Which two countries fought the Ogaden War (1977–80)?
c. What is the proper name of the Huey helicopter?
d. What post was held by the German Admiral Alfred von Tirpitz between 1914 and 1916?
e. Which organisation was described by the comedian Tommy Trinder as 'Look, Duck and Vanish' in June 1940?
f. Who said, 'My first task is to save Germany from destruction by the advancing Bolshevik enemy.'?
g. What is UNPROFOR?

Questions 14
a. Which entertainer took a touring show to every major American deployment from World War II until the 1991 Gulf War?
b. Which mountains did the Soviet Trans-Baikal Front cross to enter Manchuria in August 1945?
c. What was a PIAT?
d. Why did the Americans bomb Schweinfurt in August and October 1943?
e. In World War I, what was originally meant by chatting?
f. 'Now I shall just fade away'. Who?
g. If a World War II German soldier was wearing a cuff-title with the word KRETA on it, what did it denote?

Questions 15
a. Who was Montgomery's chief-of-staff between 1942 and 1945?
b. In which country did the Tupamaros wage a terrorist war (1969–73)?
c. What sort of aircraft was a Flettner 282?
d. Name the rival commanders at the Battle of the Falklands (1914).
e. Who were the 'Night Witches'?
f. Who promised 'The Mother of All Battles'?
g. What were 'Co-Belligerents' in World War II?

Answers 12

a. Lieutenant-General Michel Roquejoffre.

b. The Nomonhan War.

c. The M26 Pershing.

d. USS *Wisconsin*.

e. The Gloster Gladiators that comprised the air defence of Malta when Italian attacks began in 1940.

f. Field Marshal Walter Model; he shot himself on 21 April 1945.

g. An officer's tunic with the rank badges on the shoulders, instead of prominently on the sleeves.

Answers 13

a. Admiral Husband E Kimmel.

b. Ethiopia and Somalia.

c. The Bell Model 205/UH-1 Iroquois.

d. Secretary for the Navy.

e. The Local Defence Volunteers (LDV: later the Home Guard).

f. Grand Admiral Karl Dönitz, successor to Hitler, May 1945.

g. United Nations PROtection FORce in former Yugoslavia.

Answers 14

a. Bob Hope.

b. The Great Hingans (Khingans).

c. A British anti-tank weapon: Projector Infantry Anti-Tank.

d. To try to destroy the German ball-bearing factories.

e. De-lousing clothing. A chat is a louse.

f. General of the Army Douglas MacArthur on his dismissal in 1951.

g. That he had taken part in the invasion of Crete in May 1941.

Answers 15

a. Major-General Sir Francis de Guingand.

b. Uruguay.

c. A helicopter, designed and built by the Germans in World War II.

d. Admiral Sir Doveton Sturdee (British) and Admiral Maximilian Graf von Spee (German),

e. Soviet female pilots for the 588th (later 46th Guards) Night Bomber Regiment.

f. Saddam Hussein of Iraq before the Gulf War.

g. Italian forces that fought on the Allied side after Italy's surrender in September 1943.

Questions 16
a. Name the only double-VC winner of World War II.
b. What was Operation Dracula?
c. Why, in 1915, were the first British tanks given names beginning HMLS?
d. What innovation did the aircraft carrier USS *Antietam* introduce in 1952?
e. What was the name of Hitler's pet alsatian dog?
f. Who described whom as, 'brilliant to the top of his Army boots.'?
g. What does MASH stand for?

Questions 17
a. Who succeeded Lieutenant-General William Westmoreland as American forces'
commander in South Vietnam?
b. When and where did the first ever tank-versus-tank battle take place?
c. Why was the Sten gun so named?
d. What was the world's first airmobile division?
e. What did US Army Sergeant Curtis G Culin Jr invent in 1944?
f. Which British unit of World War II wore as its (semi-official) cap badge a dagger with
the letters SS?
g. Name the Czech village deliberately destroyed by German troops in June 1942,
in the aftermath of the assassination of Reinhard Heydrich.

Questions 18
a. Who was known as 'Pug'?
b. In which war did the Battle of Chinese Farm take place?
c. Why was the Bazooka so called?
d. Which former German battleship was sunk during American aircraft bombing
trials in 1921?
e. Which RAF squadron sank the *Tirpitz* on 12 November 1944?
f. Who said, 'I love every one of them. My boys were really doing their job.'?
g. In naval heraldry, what is a 'foul anchor' badge?

Questions 19
a. Who was the Austro-Hungarian Army chief-of-staff at the start of World War I?
b. What was the 'Admin Box'?
c. What was the *Volksjäger*?
d. Which American battleship fought in the Vietnam War?
e. What was unique about Emperor Hirohito's broadcast to his people on
15 August 1945?
f. Who told his troops in July 1914, 'You will be home before the leaves fall
from the trees.'?
g. To which country did the Selous Scouts belong?

Answers 16

a. Captain Charles Upham, New Zealand Army.

b. The British liberation of Rangoon, May 1945.

c. It stood for His Majesty's Land Ship, reflecting the role of the Royal Navy in their development.

d. The angled flight-deck.

e. Blondi.

f. David Lloyd George describing Field Marshal Sir Douglas Haig.

g. Mobile Army Surgical Hospital.

Answers 17

a. Lieutenant-General Creighton Abrams.

b. On 24 April 1918 at Villers-Brettoneux near Amiens, between a British Mark V tank and a German A7V (which overturned).

c. The S and T were the surname initials of its two inventors (Major R V Shepherd and Mr H J Turpin); the EN from its place of development, Enfield, in north London.

d. The US 1st Cavalry Division (Airmobile) in 1965.

e. A steel-toothed device to fit to the front of Allied tanks to enable them to break through the hedgerows in Normandy.

f. No 2 Commando.

g. Lidice.

Answers 18

a. General Sir Hastings Ismay, Chief of Staff to the War Cabinet 1940–45.

b. The 1973 Arab-Israeli War.

c. When US troops first saw the anti-tank weapon, it reminded them of a complex and fearful wind instrument that was a prop of the comedian Bob Burns – an instrument he called his 'bazooka'.

d. The *Ostfriesland* (the trials were run by Brigadier-General Billy Mitchell).

e. No 617 (The Dam Busters).

f. Lieutenant-Colonel Weldon Honeycutt at the Battle of Hamburger Hill (May 1969) – his 'boys' later put out a contract on him.

g. An anchor with a rope of chain twisted round it.

Answers 19

a. General Franz Conrad von Hotzendorff.

b. The HQ area of 7th Indian Division, besieged by the Japanese in Arakan (Burma), early 1944.

c. The Heinkel He-162 Salamander jet fighter.

d. USS *New Jersey*, as a bombardment vessel in 1968.

e. It was the first time any of them had heard his voice.

f. Kaiser Wilhelm II of Germany.

g. Rhodesia.

Questions 20

a. How did Saigon Police Chief Nguyen Van Ngoc Loan achieve notoriety in January 1968?
b. Which Italian river did the US 36th Infantry Division assault with heavy casualties in January 1944?
c. What is a ZSU-23-4?
d. Name the only RAF Fighter Command VC winner of World War II.
e. What was the origin of the term 'Fifth Column'?
f. Who said, 'The Japanese are lice on the body of China, but Communism is a disease of the heart.'?
g. What distinctive item of clothing is worn by troops on United Nations service?

Questions 21

a. Who commanded the Free French Brigade at Bir Hacheim in May 1942?
b. What was the only major battle fought by the Australians in Vietnam?
c. What were 'Circus' operations?
d. What tactical manoeuvre, repeated twice, saved the German High Seas Fleet at the Battle of Jutland (1916)?
e. Over which German city did the RAF lose 95 bombers on the night of 30/31 March 1944?
f. Who said, 'If the Führer thinks he has at hand a C-in-C or an Army Group with nerves stronger than ours, I am ready to hand over my responsibilities. But whilst these are still mine, I reserve the right to use my brains.'?
g. Which country's embassy at Prince's Gate, London, was stormed by the SAS after a six-day siege in 1980?

Questions 22

a. What does the 'H' stand for in General H Norman Schwarzkopf's name?
b. Name the forested area through which Anglo-Canadian troops had to fight to approach the Rhine in February–March 1945.
c. When and where was the famous 40mm anti-aircraft Bofors gun first developed?
d. What happened to the submarine HMS *Seal* in World War II?
e. Who was King of Italy during World War II?
f. Which German state's troops still carried the battle honour 'Peninsula' on their badges in World War I?
g. In the Korean War, who or what were KATUSAs?

Questions 23

a. Who was Allied Naval C-in-C for Operation Overlord in 1944?
b. By what name is the Third Battle of Ypres (1917) more commonly known?
c. What is an Abbot?
d. Which German battlecruisers took part in the 'Channel Dash' in February 1942?
e. Which Australian city was bombed by the Japanese in February 1942?
f. 'Success did not inflate him, nor misfortune depress him.' Who was Auchinleck describing?
g. On 1 May 2003 an invasion lasting 1 month, 1 week and 4 days came to an end. Which country had been invaded?

Answers 20

a. By shooting a Viet Cong suspect in front of television cameras.

b. The Rapido.

c. A tracked multi-barrelled anti-aircraft gun of Soviet origin.

d. Flight Lieutenant James Nicolson of 249 Squadron, for actions on 16 August 1940.

e. During the Spanish Civil War a Nationalist commander made a propaganda broadcast to the Republican defenders of Madrid stating that four columns were advancing on the capital while a fifth (ie 'traitors'/subversives) was already in the city.

f. Chiang Kai-shek.

g. A blue helmet or beret.

Answers 21

a. General Marie-Pierre Koenig.

b. The Battle of Long Tan (1966).

c. RAF fighter-escorted bombing raids on occupied Europe in 1941–42.

d. The *Gefechtskehrtwendung* ('battle turn') whereby all ships turned away simultaneously instead of in line.

e. Nuremberg.

f. Field Marshal Erich von Manstein, Kharkov 1943.

g. Iran.

Answers 22

a. Nothing.

b. The Reichswald.

c. In 1929 by Bofors of Sweden.

d. It was captured intact by the Germans in May 1940 and refitted as *U-B*.

e. Victor Emmanuel III.

f. Those from Brunswick, successors to the 'Black Brunswickers' who served with Wellington.

g. South Korean troops attached to American units (Korean Augmentation To United States Army).

Answers 23

a. Admiral Sir Bertram Ramsay.

b. The Battle of Passchendaele, from the small village which was its final objective.

c. The FV433 105mm tracked gun in British Army service.

d. *Scharnhorst* and *Gneisenau*; they were accompanied by the heavy cruiser *Prinz Eugen*.

e. Darwin.

f. Field Marshal 'Bill' Slim.

g. Iraq.

Questions 24

a. Who commanded the Trans-Baikal Front during the Soviet invasion of Manchuria in August 1945?

b. Which campaign of World War I lasted until 23 November 1918, 12 days after the official armistice?

c. What is APFSDS?

d. What caused major elements of the French Fleet to be scuttled in Toulon harbour in November 1942?

e. Why was 14 October 1943 dubbed 'Black Thursday' by the US Eighth Army Air Force?

f. 'War is good for you!' According to whom?

g. Which SS Panzer Division was known as the *Hitlerjugend*?

Questions 25

a. Which future best-selling novelist covered the Biafran War as a reporter for the BBC?

b. On which Pacific island did the Battle of the Tenaru River take place?

c. Which country developed the Owen and Austen sub-machine guns in World War II?

d. Which American cruiser was damaged by a mine in the Gulf War?

e. Did the famous football match during the Christmas Truce of 1914 actually take place?

f. Which NATO country's generals wear black collar patches?

g. What was the US Servicemen's Readjustment Act of 1944 better known as?

Questions 26

a. What position was held by Lieutenant-Colonel George S Patton Jr in France in 1918?

b. 'Rosario' was the codename for which invasion?

c. What, in naval terms, was a 'Hedgehog'?

d. What was the name of the destroyer used to ram the dock-gates at St Nazaire on 28 March 1942?

e. Name the Belgian fortress captured by German gliderborne troops in May 1940.

f. Which epidemic disease following World War I allegedly killed more people than the war itself?

g. Who said to the US War Department's public relations bureau: 'I would rather have you slip a rattlesnake in my pocket than to have you give me any publicity.'?

Questions 27

a. Name the three Army Group commanders in Operation Barbarossa (the German invasion of Russia in June 1941).

b. The Battle of Megiddo (1918) was the crowning victory of which British general?

c. What was the country of origin of the FROG missile?

d. Name the German armed merchant raider that sank, and was sunk by, HMAS *Sydney* on 19 November 1941.

e. What was the score in air-to-air combat between Israel and Syria during the 1982 invasion of Lebanon?

f. Who or what in World War I were 'Ac Emma' and 'Pip Emma'?

g. Who was sent the pithy report 'Makin taken' on 23 November 1943?

Answers 24

a. Marshal Rodion Malinovsky.

b. The campaign in German East Africa under General Paul von Lettow-Vorbeck.

c. An Armour Piercing Fin-Stabilised Discarding Sabot anti-tank round.

d. A German invasion of Vichy-France, triggered by the Allied attack on French North Africa (Operation Torch).

e. It was the day of the Second Schweinfurt Raid, in which 60 B-17s were lost.

f. Vietnam photographer Tim Page in the 1960s.

g. The 12th; it was raised from members of the Hitler Youth.

Answers 25

a. Frederick Forsyth.

b. Guadalcanal, August 1942.

c. Australia; the Owen was named after its inventor, Lieutenant Evelyn Owen; the Austen was an abbreviation of Australian Sten.

d. USS *Princeton.*

e. Yes, at least one improvised match took place. The score was 3-2 to Germany.

f. Belgium.

g. The Gl Bill of Rights.

Answers 26

a. Deputy Commandant of the US Tank Corps.

b. The Argentinian invasion of the Falklands in April 1982.

c. A forward-firing depth-charge launcher fitted to Allied warships in the Battle of the Atlantic in World War II.

d. HMS *Campbeltown* (ex-USS *Buchanan*).

e. Eben Emael.

f. The Spanish Influenza epidemic of 1918–20.

g. Lieutenant-General Robert Eichelberger, commander of the US Eighth Army, 1945.

Answers 27

a. Field Marshal Ritter von Leeb (Army Group North): Field Marshal Fedor von Bock (Army Group Centre): Field Marshal Gerd von Rundstedt (Army Group South).

b. Edmund Allenby.

c. The Soviet Union (FROG was a NATO acronym for Free Rocket Over Ground).

d. *Kormoran.*

e. Eighty-two Syrian aircraft shot down for no Israeli.

f. The phonetic alphabet terms for am and pm.

g. Major-General Ralph C Smith (to Rear Admiral Richmond Kelly Turner).

Questions 28
a. Who won the US Silver Star and French Croix de Guerre as commander of the US Rainbow Division in World War I?
b. In which country did the Dhofar War (1965–75) take place?
c. Which country trained dogs, fitted with anti-tank mines, to run under enemy tanks in battle?
d. What were found on the Yankee and Dixie Stations during the Vietnam War?
e. What type of aircraft was Flight Lieutenant R Learoyd flying in August 1940 when he won RAF Bomber Command's first VC?
f. Who sent the following message at the Battle of the Marne (1914): 'My right is retreating. My centre is broken. Impossible to turn. Situation excellent – I shall attack!'?
g. Name the leader of the Albanian Resistance during World War II.

Questions 29
a. Who commanded Italian naval forces at the Battle of Cape Matapan (March 1941)?
b. Across which frozen lake did the Russians construct a railway to supply Leningrad in the winter of 1941–42?
c. Which soldiers would use a *kukri*?
d. What was Operation Wilfred?
e. What aerial first was achieved by the Royal Naval Air Service in the Sea of Marmara on 12 August 1915?
f. What did Heinz Guderian do with the profits from his book on tank warfare *Achtung – Panzer* of 1937?
g. 'There is some corner of a foreign field that is forever England.' Where and how did Rupert Brooke, the author of these lines, actually die in 1915?

Questions 30
a. What was the nickname of US General John Pershing?
b. Which battle ended Operation Compass in February 1941 ?
c. What does HESH stand for?
d. Who was the top US submarine 'ace' of World War II?
e. Where on the Western Front would you have found the Leaning (or Hanging) Virgin between January 1915 and March 1918?
f. Which country's army wears a sunburst cap badge?
g. In which British division on the Western Front in World War I were beards permitted?

Questions 31
a. Who commanded the US Ninth Army in North-West Europe in 1944–45?
b. Known to the British as 'Wipers', what was the German name for the First Battle of Ypres (1914)?
c. In what year did the Soviet Union explode its first hydrogen bomb?
d. What did the 'Cockleshell Heroes' do?
e. In Vietnam, what was Arc-Lite?
f. Who did Field Marshal Alexander describe as, 'a good plain cook'?
g. Who headed the first ever British Ministry of Information in 1918?

Answers 28

a. General Douglas MacArthur.

b. Oman.

c. The Soviet Union; they were used in 1941.

d. US warships: they were areas off the coast of North and South Vietnam from which US Navy groups launched attacks, usually by carrier aircraft, against enemy targets.

e. A Handley Page Hampden.

f. General Ferdinand Foch to Marshal Joseph-Cesar Joffre.

g. Enver Hoxha.

Answers 29

a. Admiral Angelo Iachino (sometimes spelt Jachino).

b. Lake Ladoga.

c. The Gurkhas of Nepal. It is their traditional curved knife.

d. The British plan to mine Norwegian waters in April 1940 while Norway was still neutral.

e. The sinking of an enemy ship by torpedo aircraft.

f. He bought his first motor car.

g. On the island of Skyros in the Mediterranean, of disease.

Answers 30

a. 'Blackjack'.

b. Beda Fomm (Libya).

c. High Explosive Squash Head – a type of anti-armour round.

d. Commander Richard H O'Kane of the USS *Tang*; he sank 24 Japanese ships on five patrols before being sunk by one of his own torpedoes.

e. On top of the Cathedral of Notre Dame de Brebieres at Albert.

f. Australia.

g. The 63rd Royal Naval Division.

Answers 31

a. Lieutenant-General William H ('Big Simp') Simpson.

b. *Der Kindermord* ('the massacre of the innocents').

c. 1953.

d. They planted limpet mines on German merchant ships in Bordeaux harbour in December 1942, having canoed up the Gironde River.

e. An airstrike by B-52 bombers.

f. General Sir Kenneth Anderson, British First Army.

g. Lord Beaverbrook.

Questions 32

a. Which Japanese Admiral was shot down and killed by US long-range fighters on 18 April 1943?

b. In which war did the Battle of Hsuchow (1948) mark a decisive turning point?

c. What were the origins of the name Bren gun?

d. Who invented the geodetic structure used in the construction of the Vickers-Armstrong Wellesley and Wellington bombers?

e. Which World War I French general spoke the immortal lines, '*Ils ne passeront pas*'?

f. Which US formation wears the letters 'AA' as part of its shoulder patch?

g. What is an *Ugdah*?

Questions 33

a. The daring action of which German officer captured Liege fortress in August 1914?

b. Name the RAF Training School outside Baghdad besieged by Iraqi troops in May 1941.

c. Why was the Japanese Type 89 mortar known to the Allies as the 'knee mortar'?

d. Which British destroyer was set ablaze and abandoned after being hit by an Exocet missile during the Falklands War?

e. What was De-gaussing?

f. Which country's cap cockade had the initials 'FJI' in its centre until 1916?

g. Which is the only city known to have an anti-ballistic missile screen?

Questions 34

a. Which UN Secretary General was killed during the intervention in the Congo in 1961?

b. What was *Sichelshnitt*?

c. In World War I, what was a hermaphrodite tank?

d. In which battle was the US carrier *Hornet* sunk?

e. What was the main attack helicopter used by Soviet forces in Afghanistan (1979–89)?

f. Who said, 'Two kinds of people are staying on this beach, the dead and those who are going to die – now let's get the hell out of here!'?

g. What were 'Jedburgh Teams'?

Questions 35

a. Who commanded the US Marine defence of Wake Island in December 1941?

b. Which Allied campaign of World War I was known to the Germans as 'our largest internment camp'?

c. In the British Army, what is Ptarmigan used for?

d. Which North Vietnamese fighter ace was shot down over Hanoi on 10 May 1972?

e. What was 'Woolton Pie'?

f. Soldiers belonging to which army were issued with 'lemon squeezers'?

g. In which year were ration books introduced into Britain in wartime?

Answers 32
a. Isoruku Yamamoto, C-in-C Combined Fleet.
b. The Chinese Civil War.
c. It was a collaboration between manufacturers based in BRno (Czechoslovakia) and ENfield (England).
d. Dr Barnes Wallis.
e. Marshal Henri Philippe Petain, referring to the Battle of Verdun.
f. The 82nd Airborne Division ('All Americans').
g. An Israeli fighting formation, between a brigade and a division.

Answers 33
a. Colonel Erich Lundendorff, later First Quartermaster General of the German Army.
b. Habbaniya.
c. Because they thought that the base-plate was rested on the firer's leg when the weapon was used – a belief that led to a lot of broken thighs when it was tried.
d. HMS *Sheffield*.
e. The demagnetisation of ships to reverse their polarity; it was a defence against magnetic mines.
f. Austria-Hungary (for the Emperor Franz-Josef).
g. Moscow.

Answers 34
a. Dag Hammarskjold.
b. Literally, the 'cut of the scythe' – the codename for the German attack through the Ardennes in May 1940.
c. A British tank fitted with one six-pounder gun sponson ('male') and one machine gun sponson ('female').
d. Santa Cruz, October 1942.
e. The Mil Mi-24 Hind.
f. Colonel George A Taylor, commander of the US 16th Regimental Combat Team, Omaha Beach, 6 June 1944.
g. Teams of US, British and French agents parachuted into occupied Europe to help organise the Resistance; they took their name from their base in Scotland.

Answers 35
a. Major James Devereux.
b. Salonika, 1915–18.
c. It is a secure battlefield communications system.
d. Colonel Tomb.
e. A vegetable dish suggested by the Ministry of Food in UK as an alternative to meat during rationing; it was named after Lord Woolton, who headed the Ministry between 1940 and 1943.
f. The New Zealand Army – it was a distinctive type of hat.
g. 1918.

Questions 36

a. Which ancient Chinese strategist's works were made compulsory reading for the US Marines in 1990?

b. What was the codename of Hitler's headquarters near Rastenburg in East Prussia?

c. Which terrifying anti-personnel weapon was first used by the Germans at the Battle of Verdun (1916)?

d. Name the Japanese light cruiser lost in the Battle of the Coral Sea (May 1942).

e. Who succeeded Baron von Richthofen in command of his 'Flying Circus' in April 1918?

f. Who said, 'You should know I do not die so easily – but tell me, how were the obituaries?'?

g. What was 'Gideon Force'?

Questions 37

a. Who became the first head of MI6, the British Secret Intelligence Service, during World War I?

b. What was the German Westwall known as to the Allies?

c. For what is a Giant Viper used?

d. Name the US destroyer sunk by *U-562* on 31 October 1941, five weeks before the Americans officially entered World War II.

e. What was 'Shuttle Bombing'?

f. Who told his people in 1915 that, 'There is such a thing as a man being too proud to fight.'?

g. What happened at Kent State University on 4 May 1970?

Questions 38

a. Whose nickname was 'Tooey'?

b. What was Operation Badr?

c. What piece of equipment was known to the French Army of World War I as 'The Father, the Son and the Holy Ghost'?

d. Which foreign capital city was attacked by United States aircraft on 15 April 1986?

e. What was Field Marshal Sir Douglas Haig's middle name?

f. Which item of traditional military equipment was withdrawn from official issue in the British Army between 1940 and 1942?

g. How was the West German terrorist group the Red Army Faction better known?

Questions 39

a. Who was 'Howlin' Mad'?

b. Where were the Sandomierz, Pulawy and Magnuszew bridgeheads?

c. In which war did the 'RPG-kids' feature?

d. The sinking of which American warship by the Japanese near Nanking in December 1937 provoked an international crisis?

e. Whose Vietnam War memoirs did the University of Berkeley library allegedly class under 'obscene publications'?

f. What, to a Japanese soldier, was a *tabi*?

g. What unusual treatment was given to wooden statues of Hindenburg by patriotic Germans in World War I?

Answers 36

a. Sun Tzu.

b. The Wolfs Lair (*Wolfsschanze*).

c. The flame-thrower.

d. Shoho.

e. Wilhelm Reinhard, followed in June by Hermann Göring.

f. Archbishop Makarios III, President of Cyprus, after his reported death in the Turkish invasion of 1974.

g. A group of Ethiopian irregulars organised and led by Orde Wingate in 1941.

Answers 37

a. Admiral Sir Mansfield Cumming (known by the codename 'C').

b. The Siegfried Line.

c. Clearing minefields. It is a hose filled with explosives.

d. USS *Reuben James*.

e. Raids by US aircraft flying from UK or Italy to bomb targets in Germany or the Balkans before going on to airfields in the Soviet Union, then reversing the process.

f. President Woodrow Wilson.

g. The Ohio National Guard opened fire on anti-Vietnam War protestors, killing four and wounding 10.

Answers 38

a. General Carl Spaatz, USAAF.

b. The Egyptian crossing of the Suez Canal at the start of the 1973 Arab-Israeli War.

c. The 75mm 1897 field gun.

d. Tripoli.

e. He did not have one.

f. The kilt for Highland Regiments.

g. The Baader-Meinhof Group.

Answers 39

a. General Holland M Smith, US Marine Corps.

b. On the Vistula River; they were the jumping-off points for the Soviet attack towards the Oder River in January 1945.

c. The 1982 Israeli invasion of Lebanon.

d. The gunboat USS *Panay*.

e. President Richard Nixon's.

f. A canvas boot with a thick rubber sole and split toe.

g. They were metal-plated by people hammering in nails, bought in return for war-donations.

Questions 40

a. Who is the commander-in-chief of the British armed forces?

b. What was the codename for the Anglo-Canadian attack on Dieppe, 19 August 1942?

c. In World War I, what exactly distinguished a parados from a parapet?

d. In which battle was the Japanese heavy cruiser *Mogami* lost?

e. On which date was the US Air Force founded?

f. Who declared in 1932, 'The bomber will always get through.'?

g. Which British unit called itself the 'Saturday Afternoon Soldiers'?

Questions 41

a. Who commanded the Second Belorussian Front in the assault on Berlin in April 1945?

b. What was unusual about the Battle of Lang Vei (7 February 1968)?

c. Where were the Skoda artillery works which built guns for the Austro-Hungarian Army?

d. Who were the 'Tuskegee Airmen'?

e. What was 'The Red and Green Life Machine'?

f. Which part of the Royal Navy became known as the 'Wavy Navy' from its officers' cuff insignia?

g. What was a Morrison Shelter?

Questions 42

a. How old was Brigadier Roland Boys Bradford VC, the youngest general in the British Army, when he was killed in action in November 1917?

b. What was the 'Red Ball Express'?

c. What is MLRS?

d. Name the last British battleship to fire its main armament in anger,

e. In which year were the current Geneva Conventions agreed?

f. What was *waffenfarbe*?

g. For what did the name ANZAC stand in World War I?

Questions 43

a. On which ship did HRH Prince Andrew serve in the Falklands War?

b. What did the initials SHAEF stand for in World War II?

c. In World War I, what was a Mills Bomb?

d. What was Operation Menace?

e. Which World War I French air ace flew the Spad Vieux Charles?

f. Who asked, 'How many divisions has the Pope?'?

g. What was 'Mass Observation'?

Answers 40

a. Her Majesty Queen Elizabeth II.

b. Jubilee.

c. A parados was the lip at the rear of the trench, a parapet was the lip at the front.

d. Leyte Gulf, October 1944.

e. 18 September 1947.

f. British Prime Minister Stanley Baldwin.

g. The Special Air Service, when asked what their shoulder-titles (SAS) meant.

Answers 41

a. General Konstantin K Rokossovsky.

b. It was the first time in the Vietnam War that North Vietnamese tanks attacked American troops.

c. In Pilsen (modern Czech Republic).

d. Black officers who trained at Tuskegee Army Airfield and served in the USAAF during World War II.

e. The British field hospital at Ajax Bay in the Falklands War.

f. The Royal Navy Volunteer Reserve.

g. An air-raid shelter for use inside buildings, consisting essentially of a steel cage fixed underneath a table.

Answers 42

a. 25 years old (his record still stands).

b. A US truck-transport supply route from the Normandy beaches to front-line units, August–September 1944.

c. The Multiple Launch Rocket System.

d. HMS *King George V*, against the mainland of Japan, July 1945.

e. 1949.

f. Coloured piping on the field cap and shoulder-boards of German units to denote the arm-of-service (eg white for infantry, pink for armoured infantry).

g. Australian and New Zealand Army Corps.

Answers 43

a. HMS *Invincible*, as a helicopter pilot.

b. Supreme Headquarters Allied Expeditionary Force.

c. An early hand grenade, introduced in 1915.

d. An abortive Anglo-Free French expedition to Dakar (Senegal) in September 1940.

e. Georges Guynemer.

f. The Soviet dictator Joseph Stalin.

g. A social survey organisation, set up by the ecologist Tom Harrisson in 1938, which monitored British public opinion before and during the war years.

Questions 44

a. Name the only woman to be awarded the Iron Cross in World War II.

b. In which country did US Marines intervene on 15 July 1958?

c. For what was the Kaiser Wilhelm Geschutz used in 1918?

d. What was the 'Palm Sunday Massacre'?

e. What was the name of the most successful unofficial American soldiers' newspaper in the Vietnam War?

f. Which unit in World War II would a man belong to if his arm-badge had the initials AFPU on it?

g. In World War I, who were the VADS?

Questions 45

a. Who in World War I was known as the 'Eagle of Lille'?

b. What was the codename for Montgomery's crossing of the Rhine in March 1945?

c. What was a Liberty Ship?

d. Which ship finally stopped the German surface raider Emden at the Cocos Islands in November 1914?

e. What was Operation Babylon?

f. What was the significance of the BBC radio message '*Blessent mon coeur d'une langueur monotone.*' ('Wounding my heart with a monotonous languor.')?

g. Which former Italian prime minister was kidnapped and killed by the Red Brigades?

Questions 46

a. Which World War I French general was popularly known as 'Desperate Frankie'?

b. Where was the Malinta Tunnel?

c. What was invented by Lieutenant-Commander Douglas Taylor of the Royal Navy in 1973?

d. What was the original name of the German pocket battleship *Lützow*?

e. What is the French for NATO?

f. What identifying colours were adopted by the British Army's Tank Corps at the Battle of Cambrai (November 1917)?

g. What were 'Jock Columns'?

Questions 47

a. Which US Army officer was court martialled for the My Lai massacre?

b. Name the five D-Day beaches.

c. In World War I infantry tactics, what was the 'two-inch tap'?

d. In which battle were dive-bombers first used in support of a ground action?

e. Who was Pope during World War II?

f. When did battledress officially cease to be British Army uniform?

g. Who was the 'White Rabbit'?

Answers 44

a. Hanna Reitsch.
b. Lebanon.
c. To bombard Paris. It was a 210mm railway gun with a range of over 70 miles.
d. An incident in which Allied fighters shot down about 50 German Junkers Ju-52 transports (and 16 of their escorting fighters) en route from Italy to Tunisia, 18 April 1943.
e. *The Grunt Free Press.*
f. The Army Film and Photographic Unit (UK).
g. The nurses of the Voluntary Aid Detachments.

Answers 45

a. The German air ace Max Immelmann.
b. Operation Plunder (Varsity was the airborne part).
c. An American mass-produced merchant ship of World War II.
d. HMAS *Sydney.*
e. The Israeli airstrike against the al-Tuwaitha nuclear reaction near Baghdad on 7 June 1981.
f. It was the code for the French Resistance to begin sabotage attacks against German targets on 5/6 June 1944, the night before D-Day.
g. Aldo Moro.

Answers 46

a. General Louis Franchet d'Esperey.
b. On Corregidor Island (Philippines).
c. The 'ski jump' method of launching Harrier aircraft.
d. *Deutschland*; Hitler thought it would be bad for morale if a ship named after the country was lost.
e. OTAN (*Organisation du Traite de l'Atlantique Nord*).
f. Brown, Red and Green ('from mud, through blood, to the green fields beyond').
g. Mobile columns of lorried infantry, field guns and armoured cars, formed by Colonel 'Jock' Campbell of the Royal Horse Artillery in North Africa, 1940–41.

Answers 47

a. Lieutenant William L Calley.
b. Utah and Omaha (US); Gold, Juno and Sword (Anglo-Canadian).
c. A light tap on the handle of a Vickers or Maxim machine gun to spread the cone of fire.
d. The Battle of Ocotal in Nicaragua (16 July 1927). By the US Marine Corps.
e. Pius XII (Eugenio Pacelli).
f. 1961–1962.
g. Wing Commander F Yeo-Thomas, a French-born SOE agent.

Questions 48

a. Who rescued Benito Mussolini from the Gran Sasso in September 1943?
b. Which was the only war fought by the United States against the Soviet Union before the latter's dissolution in 1990?
c. What was a *katyusha*?
d. What was the fate of the World War II cruiser USS *Phoenix*?
e. Which type of aircraft flew on both sides during the 1973 Arab-Israeli War?
f. Who wrote in 1936 that, 'In China, political power grows from the barrel of a gun.'?
g. Where were MI6 officers Payne and Best snatched by the Germans in November 1939?

Questions 49

a. Who commanded the aircraft carrier USS *Hornet* during the Doolittle Raid on Tokyo in April 1942?
b. Which was the only major Russian offensive of World War I to be generally known after its commander?
c. In Vietnam, who or what was Agent Orange?
d. How was the British destroyer HMS *Glowworm* lost in 1940?
e. Which Hollywood director built his own Western Front for the film *Hearts of the World* because the real one was 'disappointing'?
f. Who said, 'We got run out of Burma and it is as humiliating as hell.'?
g. In the French Army, what is 2 REP?

Questions 50

a. Which British reporter was the first man into Port Stanley at the end of the Falklands War?
b. What was the original codename for Operation Dragoon (the Allied invasion of southern France, August 1944)?
c. Which important military invention was made by the American civilian J W Christie in 1928?
d. Why should RAF bomber crews in World War II fear *schrage musik* ('jazz music')?
e. Who said of the Gulf War, 'It's totally different to Vietnam. Vietnam was jungle and this is sand.'?
f. Other than Germany, which countries used the swastika as a marking on their aircraft?
g. What was introduced for the first time in January 1916 in England, Scotland and Wales but not in Ireland?

Questions 51

a. Name the US General killed by his own bombers in Normandy in July 1944.
b. In which World War I battle did the *Voie Sacrée* play a vital part?
c. For what does MILAN stand?
d. Name the US heavy cruiser sunk by the Japanese submarine *I-58* on 29 July 1945.
e. Who initiated and led the RAF's Pathfinder Force in World War II?
f. Who allegedly remarked of Field Marshal Lord Kitchener that he made a much better poster than a cabinet minister?
g. In Vietnam, what were Cidgees?

Answers 48
a. Colonel Otto Skorzeny.
b. The War of Intervention (1918–19). (Although, strictly, the constitution of the Soviet Union was not ratified until 1924).
c. A Soviet rocket launcher, also known to the Germans as a 'Stalin Organ'.
d. It was sunk by a British submarine off the Falkland Islands in May 1982 as the Argentinian warship *General Belgrano*.
e. The Dassault-Breguet Mirage III, flown by both the Israelis and the Libyans.
f. Mao Tse-tung.
g. Venlo, in the neutral Netherlands.

Answers 49
a. Rear Admiral Marc A Mitscher.
b. The Brusilov Offensive of 1916, from General Alexei Brusilov.
c. A chemical defoliant.
d. She rammed the German heavy cruiser *Admiral Hipper*, 8 April 1940; her Captain, Lieutenant-Commander Gerard Roope, was awarded a posthumous VC.
e. D W Griffith.
f. Lieutenant-General Joseph ('Vinegar Joe') Stilwell.
g. *Le 2eme Regiment Etranger Parachutiste* – the Foreign Legion's parachute regiment.

Answers 50
a. Max Hastings.
b. Anvil. (Churchill insisted on the change as he said he had been 'dragooned' into it).
c. A tank suspension system making high speed tank travel practical (later copied in the Soviet T-34 tank).
d. It was the codename for upward-firing machine guns fitted to German night-fighters so that attacks could be mounted from beneath the Allied bombers.
e. Vice-President Dan Quayle.
f. Finland and Latvia.
g. Conscription.

Answers 51
a. Lieutenant-General Leslie J McNair.
b. The Battle of Verdun (1916). It was the name given by the French to the main supply road into Verdun,
c. *Missile Infanterie Legere Anti-char*. It is a French infantry anti-tank missile.
d. USS *Indianapolis*.
e. Air Vice-Marshal Donald Bennett.
f. Margot Asquith, wife of Prime Minister Herbert Asquith.
g. Civilian Irregular Defense Groups or CIDGs.

Questions 52
a. Who were 'Squiff' and 'The Goat'?
b. Which country was invaded by Turkey in 1974?
c. What was the Leigh Light used for in World War II?
d. From which ship did F-14 Tomcats shoot down two Libyan Su-22 aircraft on 19 August 1981?
e. Who took the famous photograph of US Marines raising the flag on the summit of Mount Suribachi, Iwo Jima, in February 1945?
f. In the Australian forces in World War I, what did a small silver 'A' badge on the shoulder patch signify?
g. Name the only Luftwaffe pilot to escape from British captivity during World War II.

Questions 53
a. Which Argentine revolutionary helped the Castro brothers defeat the Cuban Army between 1956 and 1959?
b. Between which two countries did the Gran Chaco War (1932–35) take place?
c. Which German aircraft was known as the *Schwalbe* ('Swallow')?
d. Who commanded the Royal Navy's Sea Harriers during the Falklands War?
e. Who was 'Axis Sally'?
f. Which German unit wore the letters LAH on its shoulder-boards?
g. Which was the only British Empire battalion to be awarded the title 'Royal' during World War I?

Questions 54
a. What was Mata Hari's real name?
b. Where was the Barrikady Gun Factory?
c. What is 'viffing'?
d. Name the German liner sunk in the Baltic on 30/31 January 1945 with the loss of over 7000 lives.
e. Which American flying ace commanded the 'Hat in the Ring' Squadron in 1918?
f. Who said, and of what: 'First we're going to cut it off, then we're going to kill it.'?
g. What was the Kreisau Circle?

Questions 55
a. Who succeeded Montgomery as commander of Britain's Eighth Army in December 1943?
b. What did Operation Blue Spoon become in December 1989?
c. In World War I, what were 'Hutier Tactics'?
d. Who commanded *PT-109* in World War II?
e. In which war did the first ever helicopter night assault take place?
f. Who observed, at the Battle of Jutland (1916): 'There seems to be something wrong with our bloody ships today!'?
g. What is the Black Horse Regiment?

Answers 52

a. Herbert Asquith and David Lloyd George, the two British prime ministers during World War I.

b. Cyprus.

c. To illuminate U-boats on the surface at night; it was fitted to aircraft of RAF Coastal Command.

d. USS *Nimitz*.

f. One of the 'Originals', volunteers of 1914.

g. Franz von Werra.

Answers 53

a. Ernesto 'Che' Guevara.

b. Bolivia and Paraguay.

c. The Messerschmitt Me-262 jet fighter.

d. Commander 'Sharkey' Ward.

e. Mildred Elizabeth Gillars; an American by birth, she broadcast German propaganda to Allied troops in the Mediterranean in World War II.

f. The 1st SS Panzer Division, *Leibstandarte Adolf Hitler*.

g. The Royal Newfoundland Regiment in 1917.

Answers 54

a. Gertrude Margaret Zelle. Mata Hari means 'Eye of the Dawn'.

b. In Stalingrad, 1942.

c. 'Vectoring In Forward Flight' on the British Aerospace Harrier V/STOL aircraft.

d. *Wilhelm Gustloff*; it is thought to be the worst maritime disaster in history in terms of numbers of lives lost.

e. Captain Eddie Rickenbacker.

f. General Colin Powell of the Iraqi Army at the start of the Gulf War.

g. A group of anti-Nazi intellectuals who met regularly at the estate of Count von Moltke at Kreisau (Silesia); most were executed after the abortive Bomb Plot of July 1944.

Answers 55

a. General Sir Oliver Leese.

b. Operation Just Cause, the American invasion of Panama.

c. The new German infantry tactics of infiltration popularised in 1917 by General Oskar von Hutier.

d. Lieutenant (later President) John F Kennedy.

e. The 1967 Arab-Israeli War (Six-Day War).

f. Admiral Sir David Beatty.

g. The US Army's 11th Cavalry Regiment.

Questions 56
a. Who commanded the Desert Mounted Corps in Palestine, 1917–18?
b. What was Operation Nordwind ('North Wind')?
c. What are HARM and ALARM?
d. Where was 'the Hump'?
e. Whose letters were published posthumously as *A Message From The Falklands*?
f. To whom was attributed the observation that, 'war is too serious a business to be left to the generals'?
g. What is the DEW line?

Questions 57
a. Who was chief-of-staff of the Israeli Defence Force during the Six-Day War?
b. Which was the last town on the Western Front to be liberated by British Empire troops in 1918?
c. What was a Higgins Boat?
d. Which ship, launched in 1920, remained the world's largest battleship almost until World War II?
e. What was the official title of the PoW camp at Colditz?
f. In Vietnam, which American troops wore Tiger fatigues?
g. What, in World War II, were COPPS?

Questions 58
a. What was General Leclerc's real name?
b. Between which two Southeast Asian countries did an armed 'Confrontation' take place between 1963 and 1966?
c. Who, in World War I, would wear 'Drawers A G' in the trenches?
d. Who commanded the escort force for Convoy PQ17 in 1942?
e. What is a Wild Weasel?
f. Who said of General Montgomery, 'I know I can outfight that little fart any time.'?
g. Where were the Serbian forces-in-exile established after the country was occupied by Austria-Hungary in 1915?

Questions 59
a. Who commanded Panzer Group 3 in the German invasion of Russia in 1941?
b. Which ancient Vietnamese walled city was retaken by the US Marines after the Tet Offensive of 1968?
c. Who were the only mounted troops to wear body armour into battle in 1914?
d. What was the 'Baby Blitz'?
e. To the Special Air Service, what is 'to beat the clock'?
f. What unit would a soldier belong to in World War II if he wore the letters NCLC on his cap?
g. Who were the original *Stosstruppen* or 'Storm troopers' of the World War I?

Answers 56

a. Lieutenant-General Sir Harry Chauvel.

b. A German counterattack in northern Alsace, December 1944 – January 1945.

c. Air launched anti-radar missiles.

d. It was an aerial supply route from India to southern China over the foothills of the Himalayas in World War II.

e. Lieutenant David Tinker, killed on HMS *Gloucester*.

f. To Charles Maurice de Tallyrand, by French Prime Minister Georges Clemenceau, who told it to Lloyd George in 1918.

g. The Defense Early Warning radar chain in Alaska and Canada warning against nuclear attack.

Answers 57

a. Moshe Dyan.

b. Mons, liberated by the Canadian 3rd Division on the morning of 11 November 1918.

c. An American landing craft (LCVP: Landing Craft Vehicle Personnel).

d. The Imperial Japanese flagship Nagato of 38,500 tons.

e. Oflag IVC.

f. The Special Forces (or Green Berets), so-called from their distinctive camouflage pattern.

g. Combined Operations Pilotage Parties; teams of canoeists trained to land on enemy-held beaches to check their suitability for seaborne landings.

Answers 58

a. Jacques Philippe de Hauteclocque.

b. Indonesia and Malaysia.

c. Kilted Highland troops. 'A G' stands for 'Anti-Gas'.

d. Commander Jack Broome.

e. An aircraft configured to hunt anti-aircraft missile batteries.

f. General George S Patton Jr.

g. Corfu.

Answers 59

a. General Hermann Hoth.

b. Hue.

c. The 12 cuirassier cavalry regiments of the French Army, who still wore breastplates.

d. German air raids on British cities, January-March 1944.

e. To retire safely from the regiment, from the wooden clock tower inscribed with the names of those killed in action.

f. The British Non-Combatant Labour Corps.

g. Specially trained battalions of German Army attack troops. The title was later taken by the Nazi Party.

Questions 60

a. Which former Chief of the Imperial General Staff was assassinated by Irish nationalists in London in 1922?

b. Name the supply and communications route that ran from Kunming to Lashio in World War II.

c. In Vietnam, what was the McNamara Line?

d. Name the German aircraft carrier launched in December 1938.

e. What lasted from 14 May 1955 to 1 July 1991?

f. During the Irish Civil War (1918–21), why were the police auxiliaries known as 'Black and Tans'?

g. What was the Morgenthau Plan?

Questions 61

a. Name the commander-in-chief of the Soviet Navy in World War II.

b. What was Operation Merkur ('Mercury')?

c. How many crewmen had a German A7V tank?

d. Which American frigate was hit by an Iraqi Exocet missile in the Gulf in 1987?

e. What type of aircraft did Rudolf Hess fly to Scotland in May 1941?

f. Who were told at Gallipoli, 'You have only to dig, dig, dig and you are safe.'?

g. What was the ARVN?

Questions 62

a. Who led the EOKA movement against British rule in Cyprus in the 1950s?

b. What general name is given by the French to the fighting on the Western Front of August–September 1914?

c. What were 'Winnie' and 'Pooh'?

d. Which Saudi Arabian pilot achieved a double kill in the Gulf War?

e. What did 'Fat Man' do?

f. What is a Purple Heart?

g. Who became Prime Minister of Russia on 21 July 1917?

Questions 63

a. Which reporter first sent live broadcasts from Kuwait City at the end of the Gulf War?

b. Victory in which decisive battle saved Poland during the Russo-Polish War (1919–21)?

c. Which German aircraft was known as the Kondor?

d. Which naval battle was the first in history in which the rival fleets never saw each other?

e. What was knickebein ('Crooked Leg')?

f. Who observed after signing a peace treaty, 'I have signed my own death warrant.'?

g. Of which organisation were the Haganah and Palmach forerunners?

Answers 60

a. Field Marshal Sir Henry Wilson.

b. The Burma Road.

c. An electronic sensor barrier across the Demilitarised Zone. It was never completed.

d. *Graf Zeppelin.*

e. The Warsaw Pact.

f. They wore British Army khaki uniform with black Royal Irish Constabulary caps and belts.

g. A plan put forward by US Secretary of the Treasury Henry Morgenthau in late 1944, advocating the complete deindustrialisation of Germany once World War II was over.

Answers 61

a. Admiral Nikolai G Kuznetsov.

b. The German invasion of Crete, May 1941.

c. 18 (two officers, 16 men).

d. USS *Stark.*

e. A Messerschmitt Bf-110 twin-engined fighter.

f. The ANZAC Corps under Lieutenant-General Sir William Birdwood, by General Sir Ian Hamilton.

g. The Army of the Republic of (South) Vietnam (pronounced 'Arven').

Answers 62

a. Colonel George Grivas.

b. The Battle of the Frontiers.

c. 14in naval guns sited close to Dover and used for cross-Channel counter-bombardment between 1940 and 1944.

d. Captain Ayhed Salah al-Shamrani.

e. It devastated Nagasaki on 9 August 1945; it was the codename for the plutonium bomb.

f. An American medal awarded for being wounded in combat.

g. Alexander Kerensky.

Answers 63

a. Bob McKeown of CBS.

b. The Battle of Warsaw in August 1920.

c. The Focke-Wulf Fw-200 maritime reconnaissance aircraft.

d. Coral Sea (May 1942).

e. A German beam navigation system, designed to improve the accuracy of bombing raids in 1940.

f. Michael Collins, on agreeing to the Treaty of London of 6 December 1921, partitioning Ireland.

g. The Israeli Defence Force.

Questions 64
a. Who led the Rif Rebellion of 1919–26 against the French and Spanish empires in Morocco?
b. What did the initials COSSAC stand for in World War II?
c. What is a 'dustoff'?
d. In which battle did the German battlecruiser *Scharnhorst* sink?
e. In World War I, who was 'the Black Swallow of Death'?
f. Who described the troubles in Northern Ireland as, 'an acceptable level of violence'?
g. Who was Prime Minister of Romania between 1940 and 1944?

Questions 65
a. Who was appointed to command the US Seventh Fleet in the Pacific in November 1943?
b. What was Operation Musketeer in 1956?
c. With which type of weapon is Colonel Georg Bruchmuller associated?
d. In the Falklands War, what was Operation Black Buck I?
e. What did the initials ENSA stand for in World War II?
f. Which British unit of World War II wore a badge with the motto 'Quit You Like Men'?
g. What name was given to the Ottoman Turkish force commanded by Liman von Sanders in Mesopotamia and Palestine in 1917-18?

Questions 66
a. Which Palestinian woman achieved worldwide notoriety for two American aircraft hijacks in 1969 and 1970?
b. In which battle was Rommel caught in the 'Cauldron'?
c. What were H M G *Boche Buster* and H M G *Scene Shifter*?
d. What was the 'Brown Water Navy'?
e. What was the 'Guinea Pig Club'?
f. About which campaign of World War II did a young German officer remark that it was 'so like a manoeuvre that we could hardly believe that this was really war'?
g. Where in India in 1919 did a massacre of demonstrators take place by troops under Brigadier-General Dyer?

Questions 67
a. Who commanded the US Marine landings on Guadalcanal in August 1942?
b. Which two countries agreed peace after more than ten years of fighting by the Lupin Treaty of 1930?
c. What is 'Blazer' armour?
d. In which naval battle did Admiral Karel Doorman of the Royal Netherlands Navy die?
e. What was Operation Linebacker II?
f. Who said of his World War I experiences, 'I had always to remember that I could have lost the war in an afternoon.'?
g. What was the official title of Popski's Private Army?

Answers 64
a. Abdel-Krim.
b. Chief of Staff to the Supreme Allied Commander.
c. An evacuation by helicopter.
d. North Cape, 26 December 1943.
e. Eugene Ballard, the only black pilot with the *Lafayette Escadrille*.
f. British Home Secretary Reginald Maudling in 1973.
g. Ion Antonescu.

Answers 65
a. Admiral Thomas C Kinkaid.
b. The Anglo-French landings at Suez.
c. Artillery. He planned the great German 'hurricane' bombardments of 1918.
d. The bombing of Port Stanley runway by RAF Vulcan bombers, 1 May 1982.
e. Entertainments National Service Association.
f. The Raiding Support Regiment.
g. *Yilderim* ('Lightning').

Answers 66
a. Leila Khaled.
b. Gazala, May-June 1942.
c. 14-inch railway guns used by the British on the Western Front. (H M G stands for 'His Majesty's Gun').
d. The US Navy river flotilla during the Vietnam War.
e. A group of badly burned British servicemen who underwent pioneering plastic surgery at the hands of Sir Archibald McIndoe during World War II.
f. Poland, September 1939.
g. Amritsar.

Answers 67
a. Major-General Alexander A Vandegrift.
b. Saudi Arabia and Iraq. The treaty was signed on board the British corvette HMS *Lupin*.
c. Explosive reactive armour that defeats anti-tank rounds by exploding against them.
d. Java Sea (February 1942); he went down in the light cruiser *Java*.
e. The 'Christmas Bombing' of Hanoi in December 1972.
f. Admiral Sir John Jellicoe.
g. No 1 Demolition Squadron.

Questions 68
a. Which future British field marshal served on the staff of General Allenby in Palestine in 1917–18?
b. What was ABC-1?
c. Which American aircraft company manufactured the light bomber known to the British as the Maryland?
d. What country was subject to the US Air Force 'Menu' bombing in 1970?
e. Where on the Western Front in World War I would you commonly find the sign *Hommes 40 Cheveaux 8*?
f. What was the arm-of-service colour of the Soviet airborne forces?
g. Which US war reporter died on the island of Ie Shima on 18 April 1945?

Questions 69
a. Who is the 'Father of the Soviet Navy'?
b. According to General Erich Ludendorff, what battle was 'The Black Day of the German Army'?
c. What is a Merkava?
d. Who commanded the German warships *Bismarck* and *Prinz Eugen* when they ventured into the Atlantic in May 1941?
e. What did ITMA stand for in World War II?
f. Who said, 'I do not personally regard the whole of the remaining cities of Germany as worth the bones of one British Grenadier.'?
g. By what name was St Petersburg known in World War I?

Questions 70
a. Who was Churchill's first choice to command the British Eighth Army in North Africa in August 1942?
b. Where did the 'Chaung War' take place?
c. What revolutionary new method of attack was proposed by the American Colonel Billy Mitchell in 1918?
d. Which British submarine sank the General Belgrano during the Falklands War?
e. What was the 'Great Marianas' Turkey Shoot'?
f. What reply did General Lanrezac, commanding the French Fifth Army, give Sir John French about German intentions before the Battle of Mons in 1914?
g. In Vietnam, which division was known as the Americal?

Questions 71
a. Who replaced Colonel-General Helmuth von Moltke as Chief of the German Army's Great General Staff in November 1914?
b. How is Operation Jonathan better known?
c. What sort of vehicles were a Priest, a Sexton and a Bishop?
d. What was the world's first carrier jet aircraft to see operational service?
e. Who were known as 'Fannies'?
f. In World War I, which country's troops were distinguished by a fern leaf badge?
g. What was the 'White Rose Movement'?

Answers 68

a. Archibald Wavell also wrote a biography of Allenby.

b. An Anglo-US planning conference held in Washington in early 1941.

c. Glenn L Martin.

d. Cambodia.

e. On the side of a French railway car. ("40 men or 8 horses").

f. Blue.

g. Ernest Pyle.

Answers 69

a. Admiral of the Fleet Sergei Georgiyevich Gorshkov.

b. 8 August 1918, the first day of the Battle of Amiens.

c. An Israeli main battle tank (Hebrew for 'chariot').

d. Vice-Admiral Gunther Lütjens.

e. *It's That Man Again* – a popular radio comedy programme in Britain, starring Tommy Handley.

f. Air Marshal Sir Arthur Harris, C-in-C RAF Bomber Command 1942–45.

g. Petrograd.

Answers 70

a. Lieutenant-General William ('Strafer') Gott; he was killed while flying to take up the post and replaced by Montgomery.

b. Arakan (Burma) December 1944 – May 1945; a 'chaung' is a water channel through a mangrove swamp.

c. A parachute assault (planned in brigade strength at Metz on the Western Front).

d. HMS *Conqueror*.

e. The aerial part of the Battle of the Philippine Sea (June 1944), so-called because of the heavy losses imposed on the Japanese.

f. 'Tell him they've probably come to the river to fish.'

g. 23rd Infantry Division.

Answers 71

a. General Erich von Falkenhayn.

b. The Entebbe Raid of June 1976.

c. Self-propelled guns, developed by the Allies in World War II.

d. The Grumman F-9 Panther, in the Korean War.

e. Members of the Women's Transport Service, First Aid Nursing Yeomanry.

f. New Zealand.

g. An anti-Nazi student organisation, formed and destroyed at Munich University in 1943.

Questions 72

a. What was the connection between Operations 'Veritable' and 'Grenade' in World War II?

b. For what was a Livens Projector used in World War I?

c. Who or what are the SEALs?

d. What was Operation Chastise?

e. What was the origin of the term 'Old Contemptibles' for members of the British Expeditionary Force of 1914?

f. What name is given to the coloured belt worn by the British Army to identify different regiments?

g. What was distinctive about the US 442nd Regimental Combat Team in World War II?

Questions 73

a. Who commanded the First Canadian Army in North-West Europe in 1944–45?

b. In which war did Operation Karbala Five take place in 1987?

c. How did a Sherman Firefly differ from a normal Sherman tank?

d. In the sinking of which ship did Field Marshal Lord Kitchener die on 5 June 1916?

e. Which was the first war between two supersonic air forces?

f. Who coined the slogan, 'Kill Japs, Kill Japs, and Kill More Japs.'?

g. To which country was the Zimmerman Telegram sent in 1917?

Questions 74

a. Who wrote *On Thermonuclear War*?

b. What was *bocage*?

c. To British troops in World War I, what was a 'Jack Johnson'?

d. Who was the highest scoring air ace of the Korean War?

e. What is wrong with the sentence, 'Field Marshal von Paulus surrendered in Stalingrad on 31 January 1943.'?

f. Which statesman observed in July 1914 that, 'The lamps are going out all over Europe, we shall not see them lit again in our lifetime.'?

g. Of what was the Tawakalna Division a part?

Questions 75

a. Who was Lyndon Johnson's Secretary for Defense at the height of the Vietnam War?

b. Which country was defended by French troops against Libyan incursions in 1978 and 1983?

c. What was the Flugzeug 76 better known as?

d. What was a MOMP in World War II?

e. Which British Army unit takes precedence over all others on parade?

f. Which British infantry division of World War II had the apparently incongruous title 'Mountain' as part of its arm-badge?

g. What name was given to the Scottish shipbuilding region famous for its anti-government attitude in World War I?

Answers 72

a. They were the two parts of Montgomery's advance to the Rhine; 'Veritable' involved the Canadian First Army, 'Grenade' the US Ninth Army.

b. Firing poison gas shells. It was a type of primitive mortar.

c. The US Navy's Sea-Air-Land assault teams.

d. The codename for the raid on the Ruhr dams by No 617 Squadron RAF in May 1943.

e. Kaiser Wilhelm II's order to 'crush General French's contemptibly small army' in August 1914.

f. A stable belt.

g. It was composed of Japanese-Americans; it fought in Italy and France in 1944–45.

Answers 73

a. General Henry Crerar.

b. The Iran-Iraq War.

c. The Firefly was fitted with a 17-pounder gun in place of the 75mm of the regular Sherman.

d. HMS *Hampshire*. It was struck by a mine while taking him to Russia.

e. The 1965 Indo-Pakistan War.

f. Admiral William ('Bull') Halsey.

g. Mexico (Zimmermann was the German ambassador).

Answers 74

a. Herman Kahn.

b. A chequerboard of small fields, surrounded by hedges and sunken lanes, through which Allied troops had to fight in Normandy, June–July 1944.

c. The burst from a large German shell, usually the 155mm or 5.9 inch (from the contemporary boxing champion).

d. US Air Force Captain Joseph McConnell Jr, with 16 kills.

e. Paulus was not a 'von'.

f. Sir Edmund Grey, British Foreign Secretary.

g. The Iraqi Republican Guard.

Answers 75

a. Robert McNamara.

b. Chad.

c. The VI flying bomb ('Doodlebug').

d. Mid-Ocean Meeting Point: the position in mid-Atlantic where escorts from North America and the UK changed over.

e. The King's Troop of the Royal Horse Artillery.

f. The 52nd (Lowland).

g. 'Red Clydeside'.

Questions 76

a. Who was the 'Big Bertha' after whom the German artillery piece was named?

b. Which German city was the first to fall to US troops in World War II?

c. What are ECM and ECCM?

d. Which British aircraft carrier was lost on 14 November 1941?

e. Which Italian aviator proposed the idea of 'command of the air' in 1921?

f. Who said, 'We are not at war with Egypt, we are in a state of armed conflict with Egypt.'?

g. What was the US 5307th Provisional Unit better known as?

Questions 77

a. Who commanded the Soviet 62nd Army in the defence of
Stalingrad between 1942 and 1943?

b. In which country did the Mau-Mau uprising (1952–60) take place?

c. Name the only British jet fighter to see operational service in World War II.

d. On which fortress town did the first ever bombing raid by Zeppelins take place
on 6 August 1914?

e. What unusual request was made by the Viet Minh of the French garrison after the
fall of Dien Bien Phu?

f. Which Indian infantry division adopted the *Chinthe* as its symbol while fighting
in Burma between 1943 and 1945?

g. What were 'Bevin Boys'?

Questions 78

a. Who was Czechoslovakia's reformist leader during the Soviet take-over of 1968?

b. Name the volcano on the island of Iwo Jima, assaulted by US Marines in spring 1945.

c. Which famous Soviet commander developed his visionary 'deep battle' concepts
before World War II?

d. Name the three warships which engaged the *Graf Spee* in the Battle of the
River Plate (December 1939).

e. What was offered by General Sir Edmund Allenby in 1917 as, 'a Christmas present to
the British nation'?

f. Who said, of a British air-raid in the Falklands War: 'I counted them all out,
and I counted them all back.'?

g. What was the 'Blue Division'?

Questions 79

a. Name the German general who surrendered Paris to the Allies in August 1944.

b. What name was given to the Afghan guerrillas who fought the Soviets between
1979 and 1989?

c. What did the British christen the US M3 light tank?

d. Which feature distinguished most US Navy battleships during World War I?

e. In which war did Thud Ridge feature?

f. What campaign did Wavell describe as, 'an improvisation after the British fashion in
war'?

g. Why in the United States were children encouraged to save peach stones (or pits)
during World War I?

Answers 76

a. Baroness Bertha Krupp, daughter of Alfred Krupp, the munitions manufacturer.

b. Aachen (21 October 1944).

c. Electronic Counter Measures and Electronic Counter-Counter Measures.

d. HMS *Ark Royal.*

e. Brigadier-General Giulio Douhet.

f. British Prime Minister Anthony Eden in the Suez Crisis.

g. Merrill's Marauders (also Merrill's Raiders).

Answers 77

a. General Vassili Chuikov.

b. Kenya.

c. The Gloster Meteor.

d. Liege.

e. To play themselves in a propaganda film.

f. The 3rd (The Chindits).

g. British 18-year-olds who were conscripted into the coal-mines rather than the armed services; they were named after the Minister of Labour Ernest Bevin.

Answers 78

a. Alexander Dubcek.

b. Mount Suribachi.

c. Marshal M M Tukhachevskii.

d. The heavy cruiser HMS *Exeter* and light cruisers HMNZS *Achilles* and HMS *Ajax.*

e. The city of Jerusalem, captured on 3 December.

f. BBC reporter Brian Hanrahan.

g. A division made up of Spanish volunteers. It served with German forces on the Eastern Front from 1941 to 1944.

Answers 79

a. Major-General Dietrich von Choltitz.

b. The *Mujahideen.*

c. The Honey.

d. They had cage masts instead of tripods.

e. The Vietnam War; it was an area to the north-west of Hanoi, heavily defended by anti-aircraft weapons.

f. The British campaign in East Africa (Eritrea, Ethiopia and Somaliland), 1941.

g. The fibre could be used for gas masks.

Questions 80
a. Which World War I Italian pilot and author became a leading inspiration for Mussolini's Fascist movement?
b. Where would you have found 'Beatrice', 'Dominique' and 'Gabrielle' in early 1954?
c. Introduced in the British Army in 1925, what was a Birch Gun?
d. Which American U-2 pilot was shot down and captured in the Soviet Union in 1960?
e. How did the word flak, meaning anti-aircraft fire, originate?
f. Which US armored division has the words 'Hell on Wheels' on its shoulder patch?
g. From which Baghdad hotel were Western reporters allowed to cover the 1991 Gulf War?

Questions 81
a. What was the profession of 'Mad Mike' Hoare?
b. In World War II, which operation was codenamed Iceberg?
c. What invention by Anthony Fokker dramatically improved aerial gunnery in 1915?
d. Which German warship is buried in Kiel harbour?
e. When was *Adlertag* ('Eagle Day')?
f. Who coined the phrase 'The War To End All Wars' in 1914?
g. Of which war did Naval Party 8901 become the first casualty?

Questions 82
a. How did Marshal Italo Balbo, the Governor-General of Libya, die in 1940?
b. Which country was occupied by Chinese troops in 1951?
c. What was the Allies' reporting name for the Mitsubishi A5M fighter in World War II?
d. From which converted collier did British troops land at 'V' Beach, Gallipoli, on 25 April 1915?
e. Who or what is a 'Sunray'?
f. Which battle was described by Ernest Hemingway as 'Passchendaele with tree-bursts'?
g. Name the battle, fought in June–July 1944, in which over 800 members of the French Resistance were killed.

Questions 83
a. Name the commander of the US Tenth Army who was killed on Okinawa on 18 June 1945.
b. Where in Cuba in 1961 did anti-Castro forces with American support make an unsuccessful landing?
c. What was a Nebelwerfer?
d. On what date was the Royal Air Force founded?
e. What spectacular error is made at the end of the John Wayne film *The Green Berets,* which is set in Vietnam?
f. Which British bravery awards were instituted on 23 September 1940?
g. Who in the 1920s and 1930s were the *Avanguardistas*!

Answers 80

a. Gabrielle d'Annucio (later Prince of Montenevoso).

b. At Dien Bien Phu in northern Indochina; they were French strongpoints, reputedly named after the commander's mistresses.

c. An experimental 18-pounder field gun mounted on a tracked vehicle, forerunner of the later self-propelled guns.

d. Gary Powers.

e. It was an abbreviation of the German *Fliegerabwehrkanone*.

f. The 2nd.

g. The Al-Rashid.

Answers 81

a. He was a famous mercenary commander in Africa in the 1950s and 1960s.

b. The US invasion of Okinawa, April 1945.

c. Interrupter gear, making it possible to fire a machine gun through the propeller.

d. The heavy cruiser *Admiral Scheer*.

e. 13 August 1940; it was meant to be the decisive German attack on the RAF in the Battle of Britain.

f. H G Wells.

g. The Falklands War. It was the original British garrison.

Answers 82

a. He was shot down by his own anti-aircraft guns over Tobruk.

b. Tibet.

c. Claude.

d. The SS *River Clyde*.

e. A unit commander, in British radio usage.

f. Hurtgen Forest (September–December 1944).

g. The Battle of the Vercors.

Answers 83

a. General Simon Bolivar Buckner, Jr.

b. The Bay of Pigs.

c. A German six-barrelled rocket launcher.

d. 1 April 1918.

e. The sun sets into the sea, i.e. in the east!

f. The George Cross and George Medal.

g. The Italian fascist youth movement.

Questions 84

a. Which US Marine faced prosecution for the Iran-Contra scandal?

b. What, in World War II, was STAVKA?

c. From what metal are modern armour-piercing shells made?

d. What crucial work was carried out in Room 40 of the British Admiralty under Captain Roger Hall during World War I?

e. In which war did 'MiG Alley' feature?

f. Who wrote in his memoirs that in March 1918, 'our Army pined for the offensive.'?

g. At which international conference was the United Nations Organisation set up?

Questions 85

a. Which Serbian nationalist assassinated Archduke Franz Ferdinand of Austria-Hungary in Sarajevo on 28 June 1914?

b. Which country did the United States invade in Operation Urgent Fury?

c. What was the aircraft-carrier version of the Spitfire called?

d. What was the *Mayaguez* Incident?

e. What kind of World War I aircraft was the 'Harry Tate'?

f. Which action in World War II did Winston Churchill describe as 'the most unnatural and painful in which I have ever been involved.'?

g. After which event is Black September named?

Questions 86

a. Name the South African general who surrendered Tobruk in June 1942.

b. At which decisive battle in August–September 1921 did Kemal Ataturk repulse a Greek invasion of Turkey under King Constantine I?

c. What is the function of the E-8 J-STARS aircraft?

d. What was the 'Cactus Air Force'?

e Launched in 1980, what was Operation Eagle Claw?

f. What letters appeared on the shoulder board of Soviet Army parade uniforms?

g. What was Operation Bolero?

Questions 87

a. Who commanded the Argentine garrison of Port Stanley during the Falklands War?

b. What was the 'Winter War'?

c. What was the German MP38 better (but erroneously) known as?

d. What was Operation Albion, the only major German amphibious action of World War I?

e. Name Benito Mussolini's mistress, killed with him in April 1945.

f. 'It has been a good day. Our forces are themselves again and so are the Egyptians.' According to whom?

g. What was unusual about the British 35th Division in World War I?

Answers 84

a. Lieutenant-Colonel Oliver North.

b. The GHQ High Command of the Armed Forces of the USSR, chaired by Stalin.

c. Depleted uranium.

d. Codebreaking.

e. The Korean War; it was an area in the north, heavily defended by North Korean aircraft.

f. General Erich Ludendorff.

g. San Francisco, April–June 1945.

Answers 85

a. Gavrillo Princip.

b. Grenada in 1983.

c. Seafire.

d. The seizure of the American vessel *Mayaguez* at sea by Cambodia in 1975, leading to American retaliation.

e. The RE-8 two-seater reconnaissance aircraft (Harry Tate was a music hall comedian).

f. The Royal Navy attack on the French Fleet, July 1940.

g. The expulsion of Palestinians from Jordan in September 1970.

Answers 86

a. Major-General Hendrik Balzazer Klopper.

b. The Battle of the Sakkara.

c. To identify moving enemy ground forces at long range (Joint Surveillance and Target Attack Radar System).

d. US aircraft, drawn from a number of squadrons, which were stationed on Guadalcanal in 1942.

e. The failed attempt to rescue American hostages from Tehran.

f. CA (Cyrillic for SA).

g. The build-up of US forces in Britain preparatory to the Allied invasion of occupied Europe.

Answers 87

a. Brigadier-General Mario Menendez.

b. The Soviet-Finnish conflict, November 1939–March 1940.

c. The Schmeisser sub machine gun (although Schmeisser had nothing to do with the design).

d. The capture of the Baltic Islands in the Gulf of Riga in October 1917.

e. Clara Petacci.

f. Major-General Chaim Bar-Lev at the turning point of the 1973 Arab-Israeli War.

g. It was originally made up of 'Bantam' troops, under the regulation height of five feet three inches (160cms).

Questions 88

a. Who succeeded Sir John Dill as Chief of the Imperial General Staff (CIGS) in December 1941?

b. In which World War I campaign did the Battle of Lone Pine take place?

c. What is a Humvee?

d. What was the 'Battle of the Pips', fought on 26 July 1943?

e. To whom did Winston Churchill pose the question, '*Ou est la masse de manoeuvre?*' ('Where is the strategic reserve?'), to receive the answer '*Aucune.*' ('None.')?

f. Who was head of the *Abwehr* (the intelligence branch of the German armed forces) during World War II?

g. What is the name of the modem German armed forces?

Questions 89

a. Who commanded German troops in the suppression of the Warsaw Uprising, from August to October 1944?

b. In which country did the Sandinistas and Contras fight a guerrilla war during the 1980s?

c. Which World War II aircraft was nicknamed the 'Stringbag'?

d. In air fighting on the Western Front in World War II, in what year did 'Bloody April' occur?

e. Who designed insignia for the Flying Tigers in World War II?

f. Who said, 'Hot Dog, Courtney, this'll bust him wide open', when told the news of the capture of the Remagen bridge in March 1945?

g. What is the proper name of the Chinese armed forces?

Questions 90

a. Who was commander-in-chief of the Imperial Russian Army in 1914?

b. What was Operation Slapstick?

c. Which countries cooperated to build the Panavia Tornado aircraft?

d. Name the British battleships badly damaged by Italian frogmen in Alexandria harbour on 18 December 1941.

e. What unusual action was taken by the British on the death of German flying ace Oswald Boelke in October 1916?

f. Who first fought a war 'for the hearts and minds' of a people?

g. What was US Executive Order 9066?

Questions 91

a. Which former Chief of the German Great General Staff served as adviser to the Nationalist forces in China in the 1930s?

b. Against which country's armed forces did ZANU and ZAPU fight a guerrilla war from 1965 to 1978?

c. What was a DD tank?

d. What was the world's first nuclear-powered aircraft carrier?

e. What role did the RAF's 100 Group fulfil in World War II?

f. What – allegedly – were French Prime Minister Georges Clemenceau's last words?

g. Name the Free French fighter squadron that fought on the Eastern Front from 1942 to 1945.

Answers 88

a. General Sir Alan Brooke (later Viscount Alanbrooke).

b. The Gallipoli or Dardanelles campaign of 1915–16.

c. The American HMMWV or High Mobility Multipurpose Wheeled Vehicle, the successor to the jeep.

d. A naval action off the Aleutians in which US warships fired on their own radar echoes.

e. General Maurice Gametin, French C-in-C; the conversation took place on 16 May 1940.

f. Admiral Wilheim Canaris.

g. The *Bundeswehr*.

Answers 89

a. Lieutenant-General Erich von dem Bach-Zelewski.

b. Nicaragua.

c. The Fairey Swordfish torpedo-bomber.

d. 1917.

e. Walt Disney.

f. General Omar Bradley, 12th Army Group; he said it to Lieutenant-General Courtney H Hodges, US First Army.

g. The People's Liberation Army, or PLA.

Answers 90

a. Grand Duke Nicholas.

b. The occupation of Taranto (Italy) by the British on 9 September 1943.

c. West Germany, Italy and Britain.

d. HMS Queen *Elizabeth* and HMS *Valiant*.

e. They dropped a memorial wreath on his airfield.

f. General Sir Gerald Templer in the Malayan Emergency.

g. An order for moving 'enemy aliens' (principally Japanese-Americans) away from coastal areas in the USA.

Answers 91

a. Colonel-General Hans von Seekt.

b. Rhodesia.

c. Duplex Drive: an Allied tank which had the ability to 'swim' as well as to drive on land.

d. USS *Enterprise*, launched in 1961.

e. Its aircraft deployed measures to counter German radar and mask Allied bombing raids.

f. 'I wish to be buried standing – facing Germany.'

g. *Normandie* (*Normandie-Niemen* from February 1944).

Questions 92
a. Which American reporter was nicknamed 'The Scud Stud' in the Gulf War?
b. What name did Mao Tse-tung give to his campaign against the Japanese in northern China in 1940?
c. To the Royal Marines, what is 'yomping'?
d. In World War II, what was 'Big Week'?
e. From the first declaration to the Armistice, how many days did World War I last?
f. The badge of which division is the Screaming Eagle?
g. Name the German Commandant of Auschwitz.

Questions 93
a. Who replaced General Sir Claude Auchinleck as British C-in-C Middle East in August 1942?
b. In which country did the Battle of Tug Argan Pass take place in 1941?
c. In World War I, what was a 'Tommy Cooker'?
d. What name was given to the confrontation between British warships and the Icelandic fishing fleet in 1976?
e. Why was Henderson Field on Guadalcanal so named?
f. Which British Highland Regiment wears a red hackle?
g. What was introduced into Britain as a temporary wartime measure in 1915, and not withdrawn until 1988?

Questions 94
a. Which British officer won a posthumous Victoria Cross at the Battle of Goose Green?
b. By what other name is the Battle of Megiddo (1918) more commonly known?
c. In naval warfare, what is MAD?
d. Name the British destroyer which was used to liberate prisoners of war from the German supply ship *Altmark* in February 1940.
e. Which Canadian fighter pilot was known as 'Screwball'?
f. 'We had to destroy the town in order to save it.' Who reported this remark from the Vietnam War?
g. Who are the only French troops to wear a white kepi?

Questions 95
a. Which British Army commander of World War I was known to his troops as 'Daddy'?
b. What was relieved by Operation Pegasus in February 1968?
c. Name the twin-engined Avro predecessor to the Lancaster.
d. How is the US Navy's Postgraduate Course in Fighter Weapons, Tactics and Doctrine better known?
e. Who was 'Colonel Warden'?
f. On the memorial to which battle does it say, 'When you go home/Tell them of us and say/For your tomorrow/We gave our today'?
g. Which radical pacifist French newspaper was edited by Miguel Almeyda during World War I?

Answers 92

a. Arthur Kent of NBC (much to his annoyance).

b. The Hundred Regiments Campaign.

c. A fast cross-country march into battle.

d. Raids on German aircraft-industry targets by the USAAF, 20–25 February 1944.

e. 1586.

f. The American 101st Airborne Division (Air Assault).

g. Rudolf Hoess.

Answers 93

a. General Sir Harold Alexander.

b. Eritrea (now part of Ethiopia).

c. A portable wheeled stove used to feed troops close to the front line.

d. The Cod War.

e. In memory of US Marine Corps pilot Major Lofton R Henderson, killed at the Battle of Midway (June 1942).

f. The Black Watch.

g. Afternoon closing time of public houses.

Answers 94

a. Lieutenant-Colonel 'H' Jones.

b. The Armageddon Campaign. 'Megiddo' is a modern rendering of Armageddon (see Revelations xvi, Verse 16).

c. A Magnetic Anomaly Detector, used for tracking submarines.

d. HMS *Cossack*.

e. George Beurling; it was one of his favourite words.

f. Peter Arnett. The speaker was an unidentified American officer.

g. The Foreign Legion.

Answers 95

a. General Sir Herbert Plumer.

b. The siege of Khe Sanh.

c. The Manchester.

d. Top Gun.

e. It was a cover name for Winston Churchill.

f. Kohima 1944: it appears on the British 2nd Infantry Division memorial.

g. *Le Bonnet Rouge*.

Questions 96
a. Which World War I commander was known as 'Boom'?
b. Where was the 'Death Ride of the Panzers'?
c. Which British aircraft company designed and built the Roc and Skua?
d. Which of the Soviet fleets suffered a serious mutiny in 1975?
e. What was the French nickname for Manfred von Richthofen, the Red Baron?
f. Who was described by Stalin as 'a man with a very large moustache and a very little brain.'?
g. Which is the British Army's only helicopter brigade?

Questions 97
a. Who commanded the Indian National Army in Japanese pay, 1942–45?
b. What name is given to the Egyptian-Israeli confrontation of 1969–70?
c. What, to military theorists of the 1920s, was meant by 'tank marines'?
d. Name the Japanese carriers sunk at the Battle of Midway (June 1942).
e. What was 'Window'?
f. Who first used the phrase 'military-industrial complex'?
g. Who was appointed head of the US War Production Board in January 1942?

Questions 98
a. Who commanded the United Nations forces at the start of the Korean War?
b. Where did 13,000 British and Indian troops under Major-General Charles Townsend surrender to the Ottoman Turks on 29 April 1916?
c. What, to a World War II infantryman, was a 'Bouncing Betty'?
d. Name the British passenger liner sunk by *U-30* on 3 September 1939.
e. In the Vietnam War, what was Operation Bolo?
f. What motto appears on the Special Air Service badge?
g. Why were 'Seabees' so named?

Questions 99
a. Who was known to his troops in World War II as 'Ming the Merciless'?
b. For what purpose would the US Army of the 1970s have used a Shillelagh?
c. In the Dardanelles campaign of 1916, what was the 'Packet of Woodbines'?
d. Who was America's leading fighter 'ace' in World War II?
e. In World War I, was Japan allied to Germany, at war with Germany, or neutral?
f. Since 1968, which country's officers have all worn naval-style cuff rings to distinguish rank?
g. Name the French village destroyed by the 2nd SS Panzer Division *Das Reich* in July 1944.

Answers 96
a. Major-General (later Air Chief Marshal) Sir Hugh Trenchard, commander of the Royal Flying Corps and later first Chief of the Air Staff.
b. Prokhorovka (Kursk), 12 July 1943.
c. Blackburn.
d. The Baltic Fleet.
e. *Le Petit Rouge.* (The little red one').
f. Semyon Budenny, commander of the Soviet South Western Front in 1941.
g. 24th Airmobile Brigade.

Answers 97
a. Subhas Chandra Bose.
b. The War of Attrition.
c. Motorised or mechanised infantry accompanying 'fleets' of tanks (the term was first coined by J F C Fuller).
d. *Akagi, Hiryu, Kaga* and *Soryu.*
e. Radar-jamming tinfoil dropped by RAF bombers over Germany in World War II.
f. President Dwight D Eisenhower in his farewell address in 1960.
g. Donald M Nelson.

Answers 98
a. General of the Army Douglas MacArthur.
b. Kut-el-Amara in Mesopotamia (modern Iraq).
c. A German anti-personnel mine.
d. SS *Athenia.*
e. A USAF plan to tempt North Vietnamese fighters into air combat in early 1967; seven enemy jets were shot down.
f. 'Who Dares, Wins'.
g. It was a play on the initials CB, standing for US Navy Construction Battalions.

Answers 99
a. Lieutenant-General Leslie Morshead, Australian commander in Tobruk 1942.
b. It was an anti-tank missile.
c. The Imperial Russian cruiser *Askold*, which had five funnels.
d. Richard I Bong (40 kills).
e. At war with Germany.
f. Canada.
g. Oradour-sur-Glane.

Questions 100

a. Who commanded the Canadian Corps on the Western Front in 1915–1918?

b. What was the codename for the German attack on Moscow in September 1941?

c. What is a fast FAC?

d. Name the Italian battleship sunk by German guided bombs in September 1943.

e. What is the world's largest military transport aircraft?

f. Who responded to a German demand for surrender with the single word 'Nuts!'?

g. Who founded the Long Range Desert Group?

Questions 101

a. Name the first American officer to cross the Rhine at Remagen on 7 March 1945.

b. Where is Vimy Ridge, scene of several major battles in World War I?

c. Which German aircraft was known as the 'Flying Pencil'?

d. Who or what is a Pinball Wizard?

e. What were 'Anzio Annie' and 'Anzio Express'?

f. What new uniform colour was introduced for the French Army in 1915?

g. What was introduced into Britain as a temporary measure to pay for the Korean War?

Questions 102

a. Which famous war leader's name means, literally, 'He Who Enlightens'?

b. Which operation in World War II involved landings at 'Broadway' and 'Aberdeen'?

c. What breakthrough in communications was first demonstrated by the British Army's Experimental Mechanised Force in 1926?

d. What, in World War II, was a CAM Ship?

e. In Vietnam, what was an FNG?

f. Who was known to his troops as 'Dugout Doug'?

g. Who used the 'Shetland Bus'?

Questions 103

a. Which world leader was wounded by the assassin Fanya ('Dora') Kaplan on 30 August 1918?

b. Where on the Elbe River did US and Soviet troops link up in April 1945?

c. Which aircraft was known as the 'Flying Porcupine'?

d. In the Falklands War, what were STUFT?

e. Which German city suffered the first '1000 Bomber' raid?

f. What, in World War II parlance, was a UXB?

g. What was the Lublin Committee?

Answers 100

a. Lieutenant-General Sir Arthur Currie.

b. Operation *Taifun* (Typhoon).

c. A forward air controller directing other aircraft onto ground targets from a high-speed jet.

d. *Roma.*

e. The Antonov An-225 *Mriya.*

f. Brigadier-General Anthony McAuliffe, 101st Airborne Division, Bastogne, December 1944.

g. Major Ralph Bagnold.

Answers 101

a. Lieutenant Karl Timmermann, 27th Armored Infantry Battalion.

b. Just north-east of the town of Arras in northern France.

c. The Dornier Do-17 medium bomber.

d. The ground-based 'pilot' of a Remotely Piloted Vehicle.

e. Allied nicknames for German 280mm railway guns, used to bombard the Anzio beachhead in early 1944.

f. Horizon Blue.

g. National Health prescriptions and dental charges.

Answers 102

a. Ho Chi Minh.

b. The 2nd Chindit Operation (northern Burma) March 1944.

c. A radio net.

d. A Catapult Armed Merchantman: a vessel fitted with a bow-mounted catapult to launch a single fighter aircraft to deal with Luftwaffe attacks on convoys in the Battle of the Atlantic.

e. A newcomer to the unit (Fucking New Guy).

f. General Douglas MacArthur, while commanding US forces in the Philippines in 1942.

g. Those responsible for training and supplying the Norwegian Resistance in World War II; it was a clandestine boat service.

Answers 103

a. Lenin (Vladimir Illych Ulyanov), at the Mikhelson factory in Moscow.

b. Torgau.

c. The Short Sunderland flying boat.

d. Ships Taken Up From Trade, merchant ships employed with the fleet.

e. Cologne, 30–31 May 1942.

f. An unexploded bomb.

g. The Soviet-dominated Polish Committee of National Liberation, set up in Lublin in July 1944.

Questions 104
a. Which British commander in World War II was known as 'Jumbo'?
b. In what year were British troops first deployed on the streets of Northern Ireland?
c. What, in World War II, was an Amtrac?
d. In World War I, what distinguished a 'pusher' aircraft from a 'tractor'?
e. How was Hoa Lo prison better known during the Vietnam War?
f. What did the initials AFS denote if worn on a uniform in World War II?
g. What did ABDACOM stand for in 1942?

Questions 105
a. Who leaked the 'Pentagon Papers'?
b. Which major offensive was launched by American troops on the Western Front in September 1918?
c. What did the acronym PLUTO stand for in 1944?
d. Which French-sounding German submarine ace commanded U-42 in the Mediterranean in 1915–16?
e. What were 'Ata-girls'?
f. What was, 'The wrong war, at the wrong time, in the wrong place, against the wrong enemy', and according to whom?
g. What was discussed at the Wannsee Conference in January 1942?

Questions 106
a. Who commanded Polish troops in Italy in 1944–45?
b. Where was the Abucay Line?
c. Which Allied aircraft was nicknamed the 'Whispering Death' by the Japanese in World War II?
d. Which American admiral used aircraft carriers to carry out a mock bombing raid on Pearl Harbor in 1932?
e. What is the Buddy-Buddy system of air refuelling?
f. Who said, 'We must be the great arsenal of democracy.'?
g. Who commanded British paras in the Bruneval Raid in February 1942?

Questions 107
a. Which RAF commander in World War II was known as 'Stuffy'?
b. Of which larger British offensive in World War I was the Battle of the Ancre a part?
c. What is the CEP of a bomb or missile?
d. Name the dams attacked by the RAF's No 617 Squadron in May 1943.
e. Whose war memoirs were entitled *War As I Knew It*?
f. Which NATO country's aircraft roundels are red-yellow-red?
g. What was the 'Red Orchestra'?

Answers 104

a. Field Marshal Sir Henry Maitland Wilson.

b. 1969.

c. An American amphibian landing vehicle.

d. A 'pusher' had its propeller at the rear of the aircraft; a 'tractor' had it at the front.

e. The Hanoi Hilton.

f. Auxiliary Fire Service (UK).

g. American, British, Dutch, and Australian Command.

Answers 105

a. Daniel Ellsberg.

b. The Battle of St Mihiel.

c. Pipe Line Under The Ocean.

d. Captain von Arnauld de la Perriere.

e. Women pilots of the British Air Transport Auxiliary; they ferried aircraft from factories to frontline squadrons.

f. The Korean War, according to General Omar Bradley.

g. Organisational problems connected to the 'Final Solution', the projected Nazi genocide of the Jews.

Answers 106

a. General Wladyslaw Anders.

b. In the Bataan peninsula (Philippines) 1941–42.

c. The Bristol Beaufighter anti-shipping strike fighter.

d. Admiral Harry Yarnell.

e. Refuelling one combat aircraft from another, rather than from a tanker.

f. President Franklin D Roosevelt, 29 December 1939.

g. Major John Frost.

Answers 107

a. Air Marshal Sir Hugh Dowding, C-in-C Fighter Command in 1940.

b. The Battle of the Somme (1916).

c. The Circular Error Probable, the radius within which, statistically, half the impacts will occur.

d. Möhne, Eder and Sorpe.

e. General George S Patton, Jr.

f. Spain.

g. A Soviet spy ring, active in Germany and occupied Western Europe in 1941–42; it was run by Polish Communist Leopold Trepper.

Questions 108

a. What was 'Popski's' real name?

b. Which was the last British battle on the Western Front in World War I in which the Indian Corps took part?

c. In the Malayan Emergency, what was 'tree jumping'?

d. Name the U-boat commanded by Gunther Prien during the early stages of World War II.

e. What name was given to the American evacuation plan from Saigon in 1975?

f. Which German general was known as der Sterber, the 'one who preaches death'?

g. Which US infantry division was known as the 'Timber Wolves'?

Questions 109

a. Which World War I French politician was nicknamed 'The Tiger'?

b. Which war was ended by the Treaty of Rawalpindi of 8 August 1919?

c. Name the highly effective Japanese torpedo of World War II.

d. Where was Force H stationed in World War II?

e. The bombing of which Spanish town by German aircraft on 26 April 1937 provoked an international outcry?

f. 'Just rejoice at the news!' What made British Prime Minister Margaret Thatcher so happy?

g. What did the code-word 'Cromwell' mean in the summer of 1940?

Questions 110

a. Who was NATO's first Supreme Allied Commander Europe?

b. What was Operation Cartwheel?

c. What was a Yokosuka MXY7 *Ohka* ('Cherry Blossom')?

d. Where was the Zeppelin factory raided by Royal Naval Air Service aircraft on 21 November 1914?

e. To US soldiers in Vietnam, what was 'The World'?

f. In the Falklands War, what was the 'Great White Whale'?

g. Who served as Lord Privy Seal and Deputy Leader of the House of Commons in Churchill's Coalition Government between 1940 and 1945?

Questions 111

a. In which book does T E Lawrence recount his experiences as Aircraftsman Shaw of the RAF in the 1920s?

b. Which British Army rifle has been standard issue since its introduction in 1987?

c. Which American cruiser shot down an Iranian civil airliner in the Gulf by mistake in 1988?

d. How did the Luftwaffe's Baedecker Raids on Britain get their name?

e. What, in World War II, was a BAR?

f. Who said, 'One death is a tragedy. One million is a statistic.'?

g. Who was British Foreign Secretary from 1940 to 1945?

Answers 108
a. Vladimir Pentakoff.
b. The Battle of Loos (September 1915).
c. Jumping from low-flying aircraft into the jungle canopy.
d. *U-47*.
e. Operation Frequent Wind.
f. Fedor von Bock.
g. The 104th.

Answers 109
a. George Clemenceau, Prime Minister 1917–20.
b. The Third Afghan War (1918–19).
c. The Long Lance.
d. Gibraltar.
e. Guernica.
f. The recapture of South Georgia in the Falklands War.
g. That a German invasion of Britain was imminent.

Answers 110
a. General Dwight D Eisenhower.
b. An Allied campaign in 1943–44 for the seizure of the Solomons-New Guinea-New Britain area, centred on Rabaul.
c. A Japanese suicide-attack aircraft.
d. Friedrichshafen.
e. The United States.
f. SS *Canberra*, a cruise-ship used to carry troops.
g. Clement Attlee, leader of the Labour Party.

Answers 111
a. *The Mint*.
b. The SA-80 Individual Weapon.
c. USS *Vincennes*.
d. Targets were chosen from the popular Baedecker travel guides, with particular emphasis on historical/attractive cities.
e. A Browning Automatic Rifle (US Infantry weapon).
f. Joseph Stalin.
g. Sir Anthony Eden.

Questions 112

a. Which German and British Western Front veterans called their memoirs respectively Storm of Steel and Memoirs of a Foxhunting Man?

b. Name the aircraft that dropped the atomic bomb on Nagasaki on 9 August 1945.

c. What, in World War II, was a 'Long Tom'?

d. Developed just before World War II, what type of vessel was a German *Panzerschiff*?

e. Which is presently the French Navy's only aircraft carrier?

f. How is the F-117A better known?

g. Which country sent the Tiger Division to South Vietnam?

Questions 113

a. What unusual hobby had the British World War II fighter ace Albert Ball?

b. What did the initials CBI stand for in World War II?

c. What was B-17 Memphis Belle's claim to fame?

d. How was the British Medium A Tank of World War I better known?

e. What did the Challenger replace as the British Army's main battle tank?

f. Which famous Royal Navy action of World War I took place on St. George's Day?

g. How did the title Americal Division originate?

Questions 114

a. Name the Japanese C-in-C Southern Area Army 1941–45.

b. At which Allied conference in January 1943 was the decision taken to fight for the 'unconditional surrender' of Axis forces?

c. What was an Ontos?

d. What distinction was achieved by HMS *Birmingham* on 9 August 1914?

e. What was FIDO?

f. On waking to yet another grey and misty dawn, who said: 'Dammit, I'm going to have to court-martial the chaplain if we have any more days like this.'?

g. Where in June 1918 did the Socialist International hold a major peace conference?

Answers 112

a. Ernst Junger and Siegfried Sassoon.

b. 'Bockscar' (a B-29 Superfortress).

c. A US 155mm gun (official designation MIAI).

d. A pocket battleship.

e. The *Clemenceau*.

f. As the Stealth fighter.

g. South Korea.

Answers 113

a. He was an accomplished violinist.

b. China-Burma-India Theater (US).

c. It was the first US Eighth Army Air Force B-17 Flying Fortress to complete 25 missions over occupied Europe in World War II.

d. The Whippet.

e. The Chieftain.

f. The Zeebrugge Raid (23 April 1918).

g. It was raised from AMERIcan troops in New CALedonia, 1942.

Answers 114

a. Field Marshal Count Hisaichi Terauchi.

b. Casablanca.

c. A tracked, self-propelled tank- and bunker-buster fitted with an array of recoilless rifles; used by US Marines in Vietnam.

d. The first ever sinking of a submarine in war, when it sank *U-15* in the North Sea.

e. Fog Investigation and Dispersal Operation; a British invention to clear fog from runways during World War II.

f. General Omar Bradley, July 1944.

g. Stockholm, Sweden.

But the Church, with Jesus Christ as her Master and Guide, aims higher still. She lays down precepts yet more perfect, and tries to bind class to class in friendliness and good feeling. The things of earth cannot be understood or valued aright without taking into consideration the life to come, the life that will know no death.

... If Christian precepts prevail, the respective classes will not only be united in the bonds of friendship, but also in those of brotherly love. For they will understand and feel that all men are children of the same common Father, who is God; that all have alike the same last end, which is God Himself, who alone can make either men or angels absolutely and perfectly happy; that each and all are redeemed and made sons of God, by Jesus Christ, *the first-born among many brethren;* that the blessings of nature and the gifts of grace belong to the whole human race in common, and that from none except the unworthy is withheld the inheritance of the kingdom of heaven. *If sons, heirs also; heirs indeed of God, and co-heirs of Christ.*†[16]

† Rom. viii. 17

of an axiom? It is not my fault that I must deal in truisms. The circumferences of State jurisdiction and of Papal are for the most part quite apart from each other; there are just some few degrees out of the 360 in which they intersect, and Mr. Gladstone, instead of letting these cases of intersection alone, till they occur actually, asks me what I should do, if I found myself placed in the space intersected. If I must answer then, I should say distinctly that did the State tell me in a question of worship to do what the Pope told me not to do, I should obey the Pope, and should think it no sin, if I used all the power and influence I possessed as a citizen to prevent such a Bill passing the Legislature, and to effect its repeal if it did.

... But now, on the other hand, could the case ever occur, in which I should act with the Civil Power, and not with the Pope? ... I know the Pope never can do what I am going to suppose; but then since it cannot possibly happen in fact, there is no harm in just saying what I should (hypothetically) do, if it did happen. I say then in certain (impossible) cases I should side, not with the Pope, but with the Civil Power. For instance, let us suppose members of Parliament, or of the Privy Council, took an oath that they would not acknowledge the right of succession of a Prince of Wales, if he became a Catholic: in that case I should not consider the Pope could release me from that oath, had I bound myself by it. ... It should be clear that though the Pope bade all Catholics to stand firm in one phalanx for the Catholic Succession, still, while I remained in office, or in my place in Parliament, I could not do as he bade me.

... When, then, Mr. Gladstone asks Catholics how they can obey the Queen and yet obey the Pope, since it may happen that the commands of the two authorities may clash, I answer, that it is my rule, both to obey the one and to obey the other, but that there is no rule in this world without exceptions, and if either the Pope or the Queen demanded of me an "Absolute Obedience," he or she would be transgressing the laws of human society. I give an absolute obedience to neither. Further, if ever this double allegiance pulled me in contrary ways, which in this age of this world I think it never will, then I should decide according to the particular case, which is beyond all rule, and must be decided on its own merits. I should look to see what theologians could do for me, what the Bishops and clergy around me, what my confessor; what my friends whom I revered; and if, after all, I could not take their view of the matter, then I must rule myself by my own judgment and my own conscience. But all this is hypothetical and unreal.[15]

ECONOMIC ORDER

THE CATHOLIC CHURCH AND THE ECONOMIC ORDER : POPE LEO XIII

The great mistake made in regard to the matter now under consideration is to take up with the notion that class is naturally hostile to class, and that the wealthy and the working-men are intended by nature to live in mutual conflict. So irrational and so false is this view, that the direct contrary is the truth. Just as the symmetry of the human frame is the resultant of the disposition of the bodily members, so in a State is it ordained by nature that these two classes should dwell in harmony and agreement, and should, as it were, groove into one another, so as to maintain the balance of the body politic. Each needs the other: Capital cannot do without Labor, nor Labor without Capital. Mutual agreement results in pleasantness of life and the beauty of good order; while perpetual conflict necessarily produces confusion and savage barbarity. Now, in preventing such strife as this, and in uprooting it, the efficacy of Christian institutions is marvellous and manifold. First of all, there is no intermediary more powerful than Religion (whereof the Church is the interpreter and guardian) in drawing the rich, and the poor bread-winners, together, by reminding each class of its duties to the other, and especially of the obligations of justice. Thus Religion teaches the laboring man and the artisan to carry out honestly and fairly all equitable agreements freely entered into; never to injure the property, nor to outrage the person, of an employer; never to resort to violence in defending their own cause, nor to engage in riot or disorder; and to have nothing to do with men of evil principles, who work upon the people with artful promises, and excite foolish hopes

which usually end in useless regrets, followed by insolvency. Religion teaches the wealthy owner and the employer that their work-people are not to be accounted their bondsmen; that in every man they must respect his dignity and worth as a man and as a Christian; that labor is not a thing to be ashamed of, if we lend ear to right reason and to Christian philosophy, but is an honorable calling, enabling a man to sustain his life in a way upright and creditable; and that it shameful and inhuman to treat men like chattels to make money by, or to look upon them merely as so much muscle or physical power. Again, therefore, the Church teaches that as Religion and things spiritual and mental are among workingman's main concerns, the employer is bound to that the worker has time for his religious duties; that he not exposed to corrupting influences and dangerous occasions; and that he be not led away to neglect his home family, or to squander his earnings. Furthermore, the employer must never tax his work-people beyond their strength, or employ them in work unsuited to their sex or age great and principal duty is to give every one a fair Doubtless, before deciding whether wages are adequate things have to be considered; but wealthy owners masters of labor should be mindful of this—that to pressure upon the indigent and the destitute for the gain, and to gather one's profit out of the need of another condemned by all laws, human and divine. To defraud one of wages that are his due is a crime which cries avenging anger of Heaven. *Behold, the hire of the ... which by fraud hath been kept back by you, crie and the cry of them hath entered into the ears of the Sabaoth.** Lastly, the rich must religiously refrain ting down the workmen's earnings, whether by fraud, or by usurious dealing; and with all the grea because the laboring man is, as a rule, weak and un and because his slender means should in proport scantiness be accounted sacred.

Were these precepts carefully obeyed and fo would they not be sufficient of themselves to ke strife and all its causes?

* St. James v. 4.

CHAPTER NINE

The Last Things

Precious in the sight of the Lord is the death of His saints.[1]

The value of time and of life for the Christian is in the value of eternity. If eternity is not, time is meaningless. The fact that nature is the scene and the stuff of divine activity, the unfolding drama of the imaging of God in nature, renders to nature and time an intrinsic goodness in the eyes of God and of men. "And God saw all the things that he had made, and they were very good" (Genesis 1:31). Above all, the entrance of God Himself in the person of Christ at a unique moment of history redeemed time, gave it direction for man. Time and the things of time are, then, for the Christian good; they are to be loved as God loves them. The life of faith and charity is, in fact, the life of eternity in time.

Still, the vision which will fulfill faith is beyond time; the fulfillment of hope and the supreme realization of love are beyond. In time, man must live for eternity. So, too, is time the scene of the trial of man, the test of his worthiness for eternity. Through the infinite redemptive merit of Christ, man earns his eternity in time. The "state of term" follows "the state of trial." More real even than the things of time must be the "Last Thing."

Catholic belief specifies Four Last Things: Death, Judgment, Hell, Heaven. While treating of these, however, we shall add two other beliefs which fill out the vision of man's ultimate destiny: Purgatory and the Resurrection of the Body.

DEATH

The last moment, the moment of death, is a universal condition of man. It is an awesome moment even for the devout Christian, for it is that moment when loved ones are left, meriting ends, mercy becomes justice: for the greatest saint it can be the greatest moment of trial in a life of endless trial. For this reason, the Catholic is encouraged endlessly to meditate on the moment of his death and unceasingly to pray for "a happy death." In a real sense, the good life is a preparation for a good death.

DEATH : ST. AMBROSE

We know, however, that it [the soul] survives the body and that being set free from the bars of the body, it sees with clear gaze those things which before, dwelling in the body, it could not see.

. . . Let not my soul die in sin, nor admit sin into itself, but let it die in the soul of the righteous, that it may receive his righteousness. For He who dies in Christ is made a partaker of his grace.

Death is not, then, an object of dread, nor bitter to those in need, nor too bitter to the rich, nor unkind to the old, nor a mark of cowardice to the brave, nor everlasting to the faithful, nor unexpected to the wise. For how many have consecrated their lives by the renown of their death alone.

By the death of martyrs, religion has been defended, faith increased, the Church strengthened; the dead have conquered, the persecution been overcome. So we celebrate the death of those of whose lives we are ignorant. So, David rejoiced in prophecy at the departure of his own soul, saying "Precious in the sight of the Lord is the death of his saints" (Ps. 115:15). He esteemed death better than life.

But why should more be said? By the death of One the world was redeemed. For Christ had He willed, need not have died, but He neither thought that death should be shunned as though there were any cowardice in it, nor could He have saved us better than by dying. For His death is the life of all. We are signed with the sign of His death, we show forth His death when we pray; when we offer the Sacrifice we declare His death, for His death is victory, His death is our mystery, His death is the yearly recurring solemnity of the world. What should we say concerning His death, since we prove by this divine example that death alone found immortality and that death redeemed itself.[2]

DEATH : ST. BERNARD OF CLAIRVAUX ON THE DEATH OF HIS BROTHER GERARD

You know, my children, what deep cause I have of sorrow; for you knew that faithful companion who has now left me alone in the path wherein we walked together; you know the services he rendered to me; the care which he took of all things; the diligence with which he performed all actions; the sweetness which characterized all his conduct. Who can be to me as he was? Who has ever loved me as he did? He was my brother by ties of blood; but he was far more my brother by bond of religion. Pity my lot, you who know all this. I was weak in body and he supported me; I was timid and he encouraged me; I was slow and he excited me to action; I was wanting in memory and foresight and he reminded me. O my brother, why hast thou been torn from me? O my well-beloved, why didst thou leave thy brother? O man according to my own heart, why has death parted us, who were so closely bound together during life? No, death alone could have made this cruel separation. What else but death, implacable death, the enemy of all things sweet, could have broken this link of love so gentle, so tender, so lively, so intense? Cruel death! by taking away one, thou hast killed two at once; for the life which is left to me is heavier than death. Yes, my Gerard, it would have been better for me to die than lose thee. Thy zeal animated me in all my duties; thy fidelity was my comfort at all times; thy prudence accompanied all my steps.

We rejoiced together in our fraternal union; our mutual converse was dear to us both; but I alone have lost this happiness, for thou hast found far greater consolation; thou dost enjoy the immortal presence of Jesus Christ and the company of angels; what have I to fill the void which thou hast left? O! I fain would know what are thy feelings toward the brother who was thine only beloved—if, now that thou art plunged in the floods of divine light and inebriated with eternal bliss, thou art yet permitted to think of our miseries, to concern thyself about our sorrows; for, perhaps, although thou hast known us according to the flesh, thou knowest us no more. *He who is attached to God is but one spirit with Him.* He has no longer any thought or care but for God and the things of God, because he is wholly filled with God. Now, *God is love;* and the more closely a soul is united with God, the fuller it is of love. It is true, that God is impassible; but He is not insensible; for the quality most proper to Him is to have compassion and to forgive. Therefore, thou must needs be merciful who art united to the source of mercy; and although thou art delivered from misery, thou hast not ceased to compassionate our suffering; and thy affection is not diminished by being transformed. Thou hast laid aside thy infirmities, but not thy charity; for *charity abideth*, says the Apostle. Ah no, thou wilt not forget us throughout eternity.

Alas, whom shall I now consult in my sorrow? To whom shall I have recourse in my difficulties? Who will bear with me the burden of my woes? . . .

Flow, then, my tears, since you must fall; let the fountains of my eyes open, and let the waters pour forth, abundantly to wash away the faults which have brought this chastisement upon me.

I mourn, but I murmur not. The divine justice hath dealt rightly with us both; one has been justly punished; the other deservedly crowned. I will say then—the Lord has shown Himself equally just and merciful; He gave him to us; He hath taken him away; and if we are made desolate by the loss, let us not forget the gift we so long enjoyed. I beseech you, bear patiently with my complaints. For my part, I regret not the things of the world, but I regret Gerard. My soul was so bound up in his that the two made but one. Doubtless the ties of blood contributed to this attraction; but our chief bond was the union of hearts, the conformity of thought, will and sentiment. And as we were in truth but one heart, the sword of death pierced both at once, and cut us in two parts—one in heaven, the other left in the dust of this world. Some one will, perhaps, tell me—your grief is carnal. I deny not that it is human, as I deny not that I am a man. Nay, more, I will grant that it is carnal, since I myself am carnal—the slave of sin, destined to die, subject to misery. What! Gerard is taken from me—my brother in blood, my son in religion, my father in his care of me, my only-beloved in his affection, my very soul in his love—he is taken from me and must I feel it not? I am wounded, wounded grievously. Forgive me, my children; compass the sorrow of your father. No! I murmur not against the judgment of God. He renders to every man according to his works; to Gerard the crown which he has won; to me the anguish which is good to me. God grant, my Gerard, that I may not have lost thee, but thou only mayest precede me, and that I may follow whither thou art gone! For, assuredly thou art gone to join those whom thou didst call upon to praise God with thee, when in the middle of that last night, to the astonishment of all present, thou didst suddenly intone, with a calm countenance, the verse of the psalm, "Praise the Lord, all ye in heaven" (Ps. 148:1). At that moment, oh my brother, it was already day with thee, notwithstanding the darkness of our night; and that night was full of light to thee. They called me to witness this miracle, to see a man rejoicing in death. O death, where is thy victory? O death, where is thy sting? To him thou art no sting but a song of jubilee. This man dies singing and sings as he is dying. And death, that mother of sorrow, becomes to him a source of joy! I had no sooner reached the bedside of the dying man, than I heard him pronounce aloud the words of the Psalmist, "Father, into thy hands I commend my spirit." Then, repeating that same verse and dwelling on the words "Father, Father," he turned to me and said with a smile "Oh, what goodness in God to be Father of men; and what glory for men to be children of God." Thus died he whom we all deplore; and I confess that it almost changed my affliction into rejoicing, so did his happiness make me forget my misery. . . . Lord, I beseech thee, stay these tears and moderate my grief.[3]

PARTICULAR JUDGMENT

At the moment of his death every man is judged according to his deserts. The time for merit is over; a man is either a friend or an enemy of God and so he remains for eternity.

PARTICULAR JUDGMENT : COUNCIL OF FLORENCE

And so if persons duly penitent die in the charity of God (i.e., in sanctifying grace) before they have satisfied by due works of penance for their sins and omissions, their souls are purified after death by the fires of purgatory . . . and the souls of those who have incurred no stain of sin after their Baptism, and those souls, too, who though stained have been duly purged whether with their bodies or after separation from their bodies as we mentioned above, are straightway received into heaven and clearly behold God Himself in three divine Persons. . . . And then the souls of those who die in actual mortal sin . . . straightway go down into hell.[4]

PURGATORY

Purgatory is a place or state in which are detained the souls of those who die in grace, in friendship with God, but with the blemish of venial sin or with temporal debt for sin unpaid. Here the soul is purged, cleansed, readied for eternal union with God in Heaven. The suffering of the soul in Purgatory is intense, yet it is a suffering in love: the souls in Purgatory are not turned from God; they are deprived of the vision of God but they are united with Him by love. Theirs is a twofold suffering, that of privation of God for a time and that of physical pain.

The logic of the existence of Purgatory for the Catholic is found in that fact that a person may die in the friendship of God, yet not be ready for the ultimate vision of God. He may have failed to do sufficient reparation for his offenses, even though he has admitted them. It is inconceivable to a Catholic that such a soul would, or would want to, attain immediate presence of God.

The Catholic Church teaches as well that a person in life may shorten his term in Purgatory or that of another soul by application of indulgences which are given for prayer and good works. To understand this, we must bear in mind that all merit is derived ultimately from the infinite satisfaction of Christ's sacrifice. In founding the Church, Christ gave Her powers in earth and heaven and placed in Her keeping the infinite merits of His life. Indulgences are the application by the Church of the infinite merits of Christ in His suffering for the sins of men. The power of the Church to grant indulgences follows from the powers the Church claims as the Body of Christ on earth.

PRAYER FOR THE DEAD : MACHABEES

And making a gathering, he [Judas Machabeus] sent twelve thousand drachms of silver to Jerusalem for sacrifice to be offered for the sins of the dead, thinking well and religiously concerning the resurrection.

And because he considered that they who had fallen asleep with godliness had great grace laid up for them.

It is therefore a holy and wholesome thought to pray for the dead, that they may be loosed from sins.[5]

PURGATORY AND PRAYERS OF THE FAITHFUL : COUNCIL OF FLORENCE

If persons duly penitent die in the charity of God, before they have satisfied by due works of penance for their sins and omissions, their souls are purified after death by the fires of purgatory: and unto the relief of such pains there avail the prayers of the faithful on earth, that is to say the sacrifices of the Mass, supplications and alms and other offices of piety which the faithful have been accustomed to offer for each other according to established customs of the Church.[6]

INDULGENCES AND SATISFACTION :
JACQUES BÉNIGNE BOSSUET

Catholics unanimously teach that Jesus Christ alone, true God and true man, was capable by the infinite dignity of his person fully to satisfy for our sins. But having offered up superabundant satisfaction for them, he might apply this for us in two different ways, either by abolishing them entirely without any punishment whatever or by changing a greater punishment to a lesser; that is, by changing eternal into temporal suffering. As the first way is more ample and more conformable to His goodness, He adopts it in baptism; but we believe that He makes use of the second method in the forgiveness granted to baptized persons, who fall back again into sin; being forced to it in some sort, by their ingratitude in the abuse of his first gifts, so that though the eternal punishment be forgiven them, they have still temporal suffering to endure.

From this it must not be concluded that Jesus Christ has not entirely satisfied for us; but on the contrary, that having acquired an absolute dominion over us, by the price which he paid for our salvation, He grants to us pardon, upon such terms, such conditions, and with such exceptions as He thinks proper.

We should do an injury and be ungrateful to our Saviour if we dared to dispute the infinite value of His merits under a pretext, that while He pardoned the sin of Adam, He doth not at the same time, free us from all its consequences, but leaves us still subject to death and to so many infirmities of body and soul, which this sin hath occasioned. It is sufficient that Jesus Christ has fully paid the price of that total emancipation from our evils which is one day to take place; in the meantime, it is ours to receive with humility and thanksgiving, every portion of His bounty, viewing the progress of our deliverance in the order His wisdom hath established for our advantage, and for a fuller manifestation of His own godliness and justice.

By the same rule, we should not be surprised if He who shows Himself so forgiving in baptism becomes more rigid toward us when we have violated these sacred promises. It is just, it is even advantageous for us, that in pardoning the sin, with the eternal punishment due to it, he requires some temporal punishment to hold us to the line of duty, lest being too speedily disengaged from the ties of justice, we abandon ourselves to a presumption of confidence, perverting in this manner to our own ruin His readiness to pardon.

It is therefore to fulfill this obligation that we are enjoined certain painful works, which should be performed in a spirit of humility and penance, and it is the necessity of performing such satisfactory works, that obliged the primitive church to impose upon converted sinners the penances which are called canonical.

Now, when she imposes those penances upon sinners, and when they submit humbly to them, that is what we call satisfaction. But when in consideration of the fervour of penitents, or in consideration of other good works performed by them, she remits a part of that punishment to them, this is called indulgence.

The Council of Trent proposes nothing more to our belief upon the subject of indulgences, than "that the power of granting them, hath been given by Jesus Christ to the church, and that the use of them is salutary"; adding "that it should be retained; with moderation, however, lest ecclesiastical discipline come to be enervated by an excess of mildness," which shows us that the manner of dispensing indulgences is an affair of mere discipline.

Those who depart this life in the state of grace and charity but without having discharged the debt of temporal punishment due by them to the divine justice suffer that punishment in the other life.

That is the reason why all Christians of antiquity offered up prayers, alms, and sacrifices, for the faithful who expired in the peace and communion of the church, in firm confidence that they were assisted and relieved by those suffrages. It is what the Council of Trent proposes to our belief concerning the souls in Purgatory, without determining the nature of their punishment nor many other things of the sort, upon which the greatest reserve is recommended by the Council, at the same time that all those are blamed by it, who advance what is either suspicious or uncertain upon the subject.

Such is the harmless and pious doctrine of the Catholic

Church on the subject of satisfactory works, which hath been imputed to her as so great a crime. If after this exposition, the gentlemen of the Reformation still object to us, that we do an injury to the satisfaction of Jesus Christ, they must forget our having already declared, that He hath paid the full price of our redemption, that nothing is wanting to the price; whereas it is infinite; and that these satisfactory works we have spoken of do not proceed from any deficiency in this matter, but from a certain order which He Himself hath established, the better to restrain us by the salutary discipline of reasonable apprehension. If they further impeach us with believing that of ourselves we are fully adequate to discharge a part of the punishment of our offences, we can truly say that the contrary is manifest from the maxims we have just laid down. They incontrovertibly show that our salvation is a mere work of mercy and of grace; that what we do by the grace of God is no less His, than what He does of Himself by His own absolute will; and that, in short, whatever we give Him, is as much His own already as what He is pleased to give to us. Let us also recall, that what we with the whole primitive church call satisfaction is nothing else after all than application of the infinite satisfaction of Jesus Christ.

This same consideration should quiet those who take offence at our saying that God holds fraternal charity and the communion of saints in so favourable a light, that He frequently accepts the satisfaction which we offer for each other. It would seem that these gentlemen do not comprehend how much our whole being is the property of God, nor how necessary a relation all His regards for the faithful bear to Jesus Christ who is their head. But surely those who have read and who have reflected that God Himself inspires His servants to mortify themselves with fasting and sackcloth and ashes, not only for their own sins, but for the sins of all the people, will not be astonished at our saying that, pleased with gratifying His friends, He mercifully accepts the humble sacrifice of their voluntary mortifications, in diminution of the chastisements which were to fall upon his people, which shows that, satisfied by some, He graciously relents toward others, honouring by these means His Son Jesus Christ in the communion of His members and in the holy society of His Mystical Body.[7]

PRAYER FOR THE DEAD :
FROM THE REQUIEM MASS ON THE DAY OF BURIAL

Eternal rest grant unto them, O Lord: and perpetual light shine upon them.

Absolve, O Lord, the souls of all the faithful departed from all bond of sin, and by the assistance of Thy grace, may they deserve to escape the avenging judgment and enjoy the happiness of eternal light.

Grant, we beseech Thee, almighty God, that the soul of Thy servant which has this day departed out of this world, may be purified by this sacrifice, delivered from sins, and may receive forgiveness and eternal rest.[8]

SECOND COMING, GENERAL JUDGMENT, RESURRECTION OF THE BODY

At the end of the world, Christ will come again triumphant as judge of all men and all angels. This is the second coming and the general judgment to which Christ referred many times in speaking with his apostles. This belief is a firm part of the Catholic tradition.

The general judgment will manifest the mercy and the justice of God in the total history of creation. Scripture indicates that it will be preceded by the universal preaching of the gospel (Matt. 24:14), the conversion of the Jews (Romans 11:25), the great apostasy and the coming of anti-Christ (2 Thess. 2:3-4), and extraordinary disturbances of nature (Matt. 24:29).

At the second coming, the souls of all men will be reunited with their bodies. This resurrection of the dead is more than immortality of the soul: it is resurrection of man in the fullness of his nature. The human body will be glorified, according to Catholic belief, to prepare it for eternal life. "Then shall the just shine as the sun in the kingdom of the Father" (Matt. 13:43).

All men in their integral nature will at the Last Judgment find eternal destiny in Heaven or Hell.

THE SECOND COMING : CYRIL OF JERUSALEM

We preach not one advent only of Christ, but a second also, far more glorious than the former. For the former gave to view His patience but the latter brings with it the Crown of the divine kingdom. For all things, to speak generally, are twofold in Jesus Christ. His generation is twofold: the one, of God, before the worlds; the other, of the Virgin, in the end of the world. His descent is twofold: one was in obscurity, like the dew on the fleece; the second is His open coming, which is to be. In His former advent, He was wrapped in swaddling clothes in the manger; in the second, "he covereth Himself with light as with a garment" (Ps. 104:2). In His first coming, He endured the Cross, despising the shame (Heb. 12:2) but in his second, He comes attended by the Angel host, receiving glory. Let us not rest in His first advent, but look also for His second. . . .

The things then which are seen shall pass away and there shall come the things which are looked for, things fairer than these; but as to the time let no one be curious. "For it is not for you," he says "to know the times or moments, which the Father hath put in his own power" (Acts 1:7). And venture not to declare when these things shall be, nor on the other hand abandon thyself to slumber. For He saith, "Watch, for in such an hour as ye think not the Son of Man cometh" (Matt. 24:42,44). . . .

But what is the sign of His coming? Lest the hostile power dare to counterfeit it. "And there shall appear," he says "the sign of the Son of Man in Heaven" (Matt. 24:30). But Christ's own true sign is the Cross; a sign of a luminous cross shall go before the King, plainly declaring Him who was formerly crucified; that the Jews who before pierced Him and plotted against Him, when they see it, *may mourn tribe by tribe*, saying This is He who was smitten, this is He whose face they spat upon, this is He on whom they put chains, this is He whom of old they crucified, and set at naught; whither, they will say, shall we flee from the face of His wrath? But the Angel hosts shall encompass them so that they shall not be able to flee anywhere. The Sign of the Cross shall be a terror to His foes, but of joy to His friends who have believed in Him or preached him or suffered for His sake. Who then is that blessed man, who shall be found the friend of Christ? That King, so great and glorious, attended by trains of angels, the fellow of the Father's throne, will not despise His own servants. For, lest the elect be confused with his foes, He shall send his angels with a trumpet and a great voice: and they shall gather his elect from the four winds (Matt. 24:31). He despised no one, even Lot; how then shall he despise many righteous. *Come ye blessed of my Father*, will he say to them.

. . . Let us shudder lest God condemn us; who needs not enquiry or proofs, to condemn. Say not, in the night I committed fornication or wrought sorcery or did any other thing and there was no one by. Out of thine own conscience shalt thou be judged, "thy thoughts between themselves accusing or defending one another, In the day when God shall judge the secrets of men" (Rom. 2:15-16). The terrible countenance of the judge will force thee to speak the truth; or rather, even though thou speak not, it will convict thee. For thou shalt rise clothed with thy own sins or else thy righteousness. And this hath the Judge himself declared (for it is Christ who judges, "for the Father judgeth no man but hath committed all judgment to the Son" [John 5:22], not divesting Himself of His power, but judging through the Son; therefore the Son judgeth by the will of the Father; for the wills of the Father and the Son are not different, but one and the same). What then says the Judge, as to whether they shall have been thy works or no? "And before him all nations shall be gathered together; and he shall separate them one from another, as the shepherd separateth the sheep from the goats: and he shall set the sheep on his right hand, and the goats on his left" (Matt. 25:32-33). How does a shepherd make the separation? Does he examine out of a book which is a sheep and which a goat? or does he distinguish by their plain marks? In like manner, if thou hast been cleansed from thy sins, thy deeds shall be as pure wool.[9]

RESURRECTION OF THE DEAD : ST. PAUL

Now if Christ be preached, that he arose again from the dead, how do some among you say that there is no resurrection of the dead?

But if there be no resurrection of the dead, then Christ is not risen again.

And if Christ be not risen again, then is our preaching vain: and your faith is also vain.

Yea, and we are found false witnesses of God: because we have given testimony against God, that he hath raised up Christ, whom he hath not raised up, if the dead rise not again.

For if the dead rise not again, neither is Christ risen again.

And if Christ be not risen again, your faith is vain: for you are yet in your sins.

Then they also that are fallen asleep in Christ are perished. If in this life only we have hope in Christ, we are of all men most miserable.

But now Christ is risen from the dead, the firstfruits of them that sleep:

For by a man came death: and by a man the resurrection of the dead.

And as in Adam all die, so also in Christ all shall be made alive.[10]

RESURRECTION OF THE BODY : CLEMENT OF ROME

And let not any one of you say that this flesh is not judged and does not rise again. Understand: In what state were you saved, in what did you recover your sight, except in this flesh? We must, therefore, guard the flesh as a temple of God. Just as you were called in the flesh, so shall you come in the flesh. If Christ the Lord who called us, being spirit at first, became flesh and so saved us, so also shall we receive our reward in this flesh. Let us then love one another that we may all arrive at the Kingdom of God. While we have time to be healed, let us give ourselves to God the Healer, giving Him some recompense. What recompense? Repentance from a sincere heart. For He has foreknowledge of all things and knows what is in our hearts.[11]

HELL

Those who die in grave sin, deliberately turned from good as enemies of God will spend eternity in Hell: a place or state of eternal separation from God and of eternal punishment. In the sufferings of the damned, Catholic tradition holds that the most terrible is the insatiable hunger for God which will reach its keenest in Hell, a hunger which the damned will know as the fullest expression of his nature's needs and whose eternal unfulfillment he himself has brought about.

HELL : ST. AUGUSTINE

When God punishes sinners, He does not inflict His evil on them, but leaves them to their own evil. "Behold," saith the Psalmist, "he hath been in labour with injustice, he hath conceived toil; brought forth iniquity. He hath opened a pit and dug it: and he is fallen into the hole he made. His sorrow shall be turned on his own head: and his iniquity shall come down upon his crown" (Ps. vii, 15 *sqq.*).[12]

To be gone from the kingdom of God, to be an exile from God's city, to be cut off from the divine life, to be without the manifold sweetness of God . . . is so mighty a punishment that no torments that we know can be compared with it.[13]

HELL : ROBERT CARDINAL BELLARMINE

It remaineth that we consider the justice which God will use in punishing sinners in the uttermost depths of hell. Wherefore if we mark with attention and diligence, we shall indeed understand that it is most true which the Apostle teaches "It is a fearful thing to fall into the hands of the living God" (Heb. 10:31).

For God the just judge will punish all sins though ever so small, as, for example, an idle word, for so we read in the Gospel: "Every idle word that men shall speak, they shall render an account of it in the day of judgment" (Matt. 12:36).

Neither shall all sins be punished only, but so horribly punished that scarcely any man can imagine it. For as no eye hath seen, nor ear heard; neither hath it entered into the heart of man, what things God hath prepared for them that love him (1 Cor. 2:9), so no eye hath seen nor ear heard, neither has it entered into the heart of man what things God has prepared for those who hate him.

The punishments of sinners in hell shall be very great, very many and very pure, to wit, mixed with no comforts and which shall increase their misery everlasting. They shall be many because every power of the soul and every sense shall be tormented. Weigh the words of the highest Judge's sentence "Get ye away from me, ye cursed, into everlasting fire which has been prepared for the devil and his angels" (Matt. 25:41). Get ye away, He saith, depart ye from the company of the blessed, being forever deprived of the sight of God, which is the highest essential happiness and best end for which you were created. *Ye cursed*, He saith, that is, hope not hereafter for any benediction for ye are deprived of the life of grace and all hope of salvation; the water of wisdom and dew of divine inspiration shall not rain upon you; the beams of heavenly light shall not shine upon you; neither the grace of repentance nor the flower of charity, nor the fruits of good works shall grow in you. Neither shall ye lose only spiritual and eternal goods, but also corporal and temporal; ye shall have no riches, no delights, no comforts, but shall be like the fig tree which being cursed by me withered from the root all over (Matt. 21:19). *Into fire*, that is, into the furnace of burning and unquenchable fire (Matt. 13:42) which shall not consume one member alone but all the members together with horrible punishment. *Everlasting*, that is, into a fire which is blown by the breath of the Almighty and therefore needeth no fuel to make it always to burn, that as your fault shall still remain, so your punishment shall forever endure. Therefore I can truly exclaim "Which of you can dwell with devouring fire? Which of you shall dwell with everlasting burnings?" (Isa. 33:14). For there shall be the worm of conscience and remembrance of this life wherein they might easily, if they would, have escaped their punishment and obtained eternal joys. . . .

But if all these things which we have said of the loss of all goods both celestial and terrestrial and of most unsufferable dolours, ignominies and disgraces were to have end, or at least some kind of comfort or mitigation as all miseries in this life have, they might in some sort be thought tolerable; but since it is most certain and undeniable that the happiness of the blessed shall continue forever without mixture of misery, so likewise shall the unhappiness of the damned continue forever without mixture of comfort.

Lastly, if the sin of the damned were not eternal, we might marvel that the punishment thereof should be eternal but seeing that the obstinacy of the damned is eternal, why should we wonder if their punishment is also eternal? And this wilful obstinacy in wickedness, which is in both the damned and the devils, I say, this perverse will, which is in them averted from God the chief happiness, and shall so forever remain, maketh holy men more to fear a mortal sin than hell fire.[14]

HEAVEN

Those who die in the love and friendship of God enjoy forever the face-to-face vision of God. The soul and God are united in an act of love: vision fills the mind, love engages the will, there is born perfect and unceasing joy in union with the supreme Good for which all nature yearns. "Eye hath not seen, nor ear heard, neither hath it entered into the heart of man, what things God has prepared for them that love him" (1 Cor. 2:9).

THE JOY OF HEAVEN : POPE BENEDICT XII

Those who after the ascension of Our Savior Jesus Christ into heaven have died or shall have died, have been, are and shall be in heaven, in the kingdom of the heavens, in the celestial paradise with Christ and joined to the company of the holy angels . . . And they see the divine essence with intuitive, even with face-to-face vision, with no creature thrusting itself in between by means of which they might be able to see, but with the divine essence showing itself to them directly, unveiled and clear. And so, after this manner of vision, they enjoy the same divine essence. And moreover it is on account of this very vision and this very enjoyment that the souls of those who have passed from this life are truly happy; and they have rest and life everlasting.[15]

ETERNAL PEACE : ST. AUGUSTINE

Peace there will be there, perfect peace will be there. Where thou wishest thou shalt be, but from God thou wilt not depart. Where thou wishest thou shalt be, but wherever thou goest thou shalt have thy God. With Him, from whom thou art blessed, shalt thou ever be.[16]

THE VISION OF PARADISE : THE APOCALYPSE

And I saw a new heaven and a new earth. For the first heaven and the first earth was gone: and the sea is now no more.

And I, John, saw the holy city, the new Jerusalem, coming down out of heaven from God, prepared as a bride adorned for her husband.

And I heard a great voice from the throne, saying: Behold the tabernacle of God with men: and he will dwell with them. And they shall be his people: and God himself with them shall be their God.

And God shall wipe away all tears from their eyes: and death shall be no more. Nor mourning, nor crying, nor sorrow shall be any more: for the former things are passed away. . . .

And he said to me: It is done. I am Alpha and Omega: the Beginning and the End. To him that thirsteth I will give of the fountain of the water of life, freely.

He that shall overcome shall possess these things. And I will be his God: and he shall be my son. . . .

And there came one of the seven angels, who had the vials full of the seven last plagues, and spoke with me saying: Come and I will shew thee the bride, the wife of the Lamb.

And he took me up in spirit to a great and high mountain: and he shewed me the holy city Jerusalem, coming down out of heaven from God.

Having the glory of God. And the light thereof was like to a precious stone, as to the jasper stone even as crystal.

And it had a wall great and high, having twelve gates, and

in the gates twelve angels, and names written thereon, which are the names of the twelve tribes of the children of Israel. . . .

And the wall of the city had twelve foundations: and in them, the twelve names of the twelve apostles of the Lamb. . . .

And I saw no temple therein. For the Lord God Almighty is the temple thereof, and the Lamb.

And the city hath no need of the sun, nor of the moon, to shine in it. For the glory of God hath enlightened it: and the Lamb is the lamp thereof.

And the nations shall walk in the light of it: and the kings of the earth shall bring their glory and honor into it.

And the gates thereof shall not be shut by day: for there shall be no night there.

And they shall bring the glory and honour of nations into it.

There shall not enter into it any thing defiled or that worketh abomination or maketh a lie: but they that are written in the book of life of the Lamb. . . .

And they shall see his face: and his name shall be on their foreheads.[17]

References
and
Index of Sources

References

Standard references used in the preparation of this work are referred to in the references by the following symbols:

[LF]   *Library of the Fathers of the Holy Catholic Church,* ed., E. P. Pusey, J. H. Newman, J. Keble, and C. Merriot (Oxford: J. H. Parker, 1838–85).

[AN]   *The Anti-Nicene Fathers,* ed. Rev. Alexander Roberts, D.D., and James Donaldson, L.L.D. (Buffalo: The Christian Literature Publishing Company, 1885–96).

[NF]   *A Select Library of the Nicene and Post-Nicene Fathers of the Christian Church,* ed. Philip Schaff (Buffalo: The Christian Literature Publishing Company, 1886–90).

[NF2]   *A Select Library of the Nicene and Post-Nicene Fathers of the Christian Church,* ed., Philip Schaff, D.D. and Henry Wace, D.D. Second Series (Buffalo: The Christian Literature Publishing Company, 1890–94).

[TM]   *St. Augustine,* Sir Toby Matthew's translation, ed. by Dom Roger Hudleston, O.S.B. (1620).

Biblical references are given from the Douay version.
Editor's translations are so indicated.

CHAPTER I

1. Wisdom 2:5.
2. Eccl. 3:1–9.
3. St. Augustine, *Enarationes in Psalmos,* XXXVIII, 7 (LF).
4. St. Augustine, *Sermo* XVII, vii, 7 (LF).
5. St. Augustine, *Enarrationes in Psalmos,* XLI, 13 (LF).
6. Eccl. 1:2–10, 14–15.
7. Job 8:11–15; 14:1–2.
8. Wisdom 3:11; 2:1–5.
9. St. John Chrysostom, *The Vanity of the World* (NF).
10. Ps. 41:2–5, 12.
11. St. Augustine, *Confessions,* I, i, 1; VII, viii, 16; X, xxvii, 38 (TM).

CHAPTER II

1. Ps. 18:1.
2. St. Anselm, *Proslogion,* 1, (ed. tr.).
3. Henry Edward Manning, *The Vatican Council* (New York, 1871) I, 209.
4. St. Anselm, *op. cit.*
5. St. Bonaventure, *Itinerarium* III (ed. tr.).
6. Wisdom 13:1–3.
7. Romans 1:20–25.

8. St. Augustine, *Sermo* CCXLI, ii, 2; iii, 3 (LF).
9. St. Thomas Aquinas, *Summa Theologiae*, I, q. 2, a. 3 (ed. tr.).
10. John Henry Newman, *A Grammar of Assent* (London, 1870), ch. V.
11. St. Augustine, *In Joannis Evangelium tractatus* XIII, 5 (LF).
12. St. Augustine, *Sermo* LII, vi, 16 (LF).
13. St. Augustine, *Confessions*, X, vi, 8 (TM).
14. Manning, *op. cit.*, Constitution *"Dei Filius,"* I.
15. St. Bonaventure, *Itinerarium*, V (ed. tr.).
16. St. Augustine, *Confessions*, XI, xiii, 16 (TM).
17. St. Augustine, *The City of God*, XI, 4–6 (NF).
18. Pius XII, Encyclical, *Humani Generis*, authorized English translation.
19. Matt. 6:25–34.
20. St. John Damascene, *Exposition of the Orthodox Faith* (NF2).

7. Gen. 3:22–24.
8. St. Anselm, *De conceptione virginis et peccato originali*, c. 27, cited in Chetwood, *op. cit.*
9. Cited in *ibid.*
10. St. Thomas Aquinas, *Summa theologiae* I, ii, q. 82, a. 3 (ed. tr.).
11. *The Canons and Decrees of the Sacred and Ecumenical Council of Trent* (London: Burns Oates; New York: Catholic Publication Society, 1848), Sess. V., D. 789.
12. John Henry Newman, *Apologia pro Vita Sua* (London, 1864), ch. V.
13. Lamentations 5:1–7, 15–22.
14. Romans 7:14–25.
15. Isa. 11:1–5.
16. Isa. 35:1–4.
17. Isa. 7:14.
18. Isa. 40:10–11.
19. Isa. 45:8.
20. Ps. 129.
21. Luke 3:2–6.
22. Selections from the Liturgy for Advent.

CHAPTER III

1. Isa. 11:1.
2. Pius XII, Encyclical, *Humani Generis*, authorized English translation.
3. John Henry Newman, *A Grammar of Assent*, ch. V.
4. Origen, *On Prayer* (AN).
5. Hugh of St. Victor, *Expositio in Hierarchiam caelestem* IV (ed. tr.).
6. St. John Damascene, *De Fide Orthodoxi*, L. 2, c. 30, cited in Thomas B. Chetwood, S. J., *God and Creation* (New York: Benziger Bros., 1928).

CHAPTER IV

1. John 1:1–14.
2. Martyrology for the Feast of the Nativity, *The Breviary* (Edinburgh and London: Wm. Blackwood and Sons, 1879).
3. Dionysius of Rome, *Quicumque vult* (AN).
4. St. Augustine, *Epistle* CCXXXII, 5, 6 (NF).
5. Pope Leo XIII, Encyclical *"Divinum Illud,"* in John Wynne, *The Great Encyclical Letters of Pope Leo XIII* (New York, 1903).

6. Gen. 3:12–15.
7. Luke 1:46–55.
8. Apoc. 12:1–2; 5–9; 13–17.
9. St. Bernard, Homily on *"Missus Est,"* standard translation, cited in George N. Shuster, *Treasury of Catholic Literature* (New York, 1943).
10. Common Prayer of the Church.
11. St. Cyril of Alexandria, *Epistle to Bishop Nestorius with Twelve Anathematisms* (NF2).
12. Pius IX, Papal bull, *Ineffabilis Deus,* December 8, 1864.
13. Pius XII, Apostolic Constitution, *Munificentissimus Deus,* November 2, 1950.
14. St. Augustine, *Epistle* CII, ii, 12, 15 (NF).
15. St. Gregory Nazianzen, *Oration* XXVIII (NF2).
16. Luke 2:6–12.
17. St. Augustine, *Sermo* CXC, iii, 4 (LF).
18. St. Bernard, "Sermon for the Feast of the Nativity," *Oeuvres Complètes de St. Bernard,* trans. Abbés Dion et Charpentier (Paris, 1867), (ed. tr.).
19. Matt. 11:28.
20. Luke 21:16–19.
21. Mark 8:34–38.
22. Matt. 5:17–19.
23. *Ibid.,* 21–24.
24. *Ibid.,* 38–41.
25. *Ibid.,* 43–48.
26. *Ibid.,* 2–12.
27. Mark 14:61–62.
28. John 8:52–59.
29. John 14:8–10.
30. Matt. 27:41–43.
31. Mark 10:32–34.
32. Matt. 26:21–25.
33. Luke 19:41–44.
34. Matt. 9:2–7.
35. Mark 6:38–44.
36. Mark 14:22–25.
37. Isa. 53:2–7.
38. Matt. 27:31–54, *passim.*
39. "Reproaches sung on Good Friday," *The Breviary.*
40. St. Cyril of Jerusalem, *Catechetical Lecture* XIII (NF2).
41. Matt. 28:5–10.
42. *Exultet:* Hymn from the Blessing of the Paschal Candle.
43. St. John Vianney, Sermon for Easter Sunday, *Sermons for Sundays and Feasts of the Year* (New York: Joseph Wagner, 1901).

CHAPTER V

1. John 10:16.
2. John 15:5.
3. John 10:16.
4. Matt. 16:17–19.
5. Matt. 28:18–19.
6. Luke 10:16.
7. John 14:16–18.
8. John 14:26.
9. Acts 2:3–4.
10. I Cor. 12:12–31.
11. Pius XII, Encyclical, *Mystici Corporis,* Official English Version, Vatican Polyglot Edition, 1943.
12. Leo XIII, Encyclical, *Satis Cogitum,* in John Wynne, *Great Encyclical Letters of Pope Leo XIII* (New York, 1903).
13. Luke 12:33.
14. I Cor. 3:8.
15. Council of Trent, *op. cit.,* Sess. VI, ch. 16.
16. St. John Chrysostom, *Homily XXIII on Gospel of St. Matthew* (NF).
17. St. Augustine, *Enarrationes in Psalmos,* CXXX, 1 (LF).
18. John 3:3–5.

19. John 15:26.
20. Acts 8:14–17.
21. John 6:48–59.
22. Matt. 16:19.
23. John 20:22–23.
24. Rite of the Sacrament of Penance, *Roman Ritual.*
25. St. John Chrysostom, *On The Priesthood,* n. 6 (NF).
26. John Henry Newman, "Christ the High Priest," *Public and Parochial Sermons,* Vol. VI.
27. Mark 10:6–9.
28. Eph. 5:22–32.
29. St. Augustine, *De Civitate Dei,* X, vi (NF).
30. Council of Trent, *op. cit.,* Sess. XXII, ch. 1.
31. St. Cyprian, *Letter to Caecilius* (AN).
32. *Mass for the Feast of the Holy Trinity,* standard trans.
33. St. Chromatus, *Tracts on the Gospel of St. Matthew,* viii, cited in Joseph Berrington, *The Faith of Catholics* (New York, 1851), Vol. II.
34. St. John Chrysostom, *Homilies on First Epistle to the Corinthians* (NF).
35. St. Cyril of Jerusalem, *Catechetical Lecture* (NF2).
36. Manning, *op. cit.,* Vatican Council, Sess. IV, ch. iv.
37. Pope St. Leo I, *Sermon on Anniversary of His Elevation to the Episcopate* (NF).
38. St. Gregory Nazianzen, *Tract on Origen,* 26, cited in Berrington, *op. cit.*
39. Sacred Congregation of the Council, *Acta Apostolica Sedis* 38–401, authorized English translation, Oct. 14, 1946.
40. Supreme Sacred Congregation of the Holy Office, Decree of July 28, 1949, authorized English translation.

CHAPTER VI

1. I John 5:4.
2. Mark 16:15–16.
3. John 20:27–29.
4. Romans 1:16–17.
5. I John 5:3–5.
6. *Council of Trent, op. cit.,* Sess. VI, ch. 6.
7. St. Augustine, *Sermo* XXXVIII, ii, 3 (LF).
8. St. Augustine, *Sermo* XLIII, i, 1 (LF).
9. Hebr. 11:1–6.
10. Manning, *op. cit.* Vatican Council, Sess. III.
11. St. Augustine, *De ordini libri* II, ix, 26, 27 (TM).
12. Irenaeus, *Adversus Heresias,* I, i, 1 (AN).
13. *The Creed of the Apostles,* Common Prayer of the Church.
14. *The Creed of the Council of Nicaea,* 325 A.D., revised by Council of Constantinople, 381 A.D. (NF2).
15. John Henry Newman, "Faith Is a Gift of God," *Discourses to Mixed Congregations* (London, 1887).
16. St. Augustine, *De spiritu et littera,* xxi, 54; xxxiv, 60 (NF).
17. John Henry Newman, *Grammar of Assent,* ch. V.
18. Common Prayers of the Church.

CHAPTER VII

1. Gal. 2:20.
2. Matt. 7:13–14.
3. Matt. 6:20–21.

4. John 15:9-10; 12–14.
5. I Cor. 13.
6. St. Augustine, *De gratia Christi*, XXVI, 27 (NF).
7. St. Augustine, *Contra Julianum*, IV, iii, 33 (TM).
8. St. Augustine, *In Epistulam Joannis ad Parthos*, Tr. vii, 8 (LF).
9. St. Francis de Sales, *A Treatise on Love of God* (New York: P. O'Shea, 1868).
10. St. Augustine, *Enarrationes in Psalmos*, CI, i, 3 (LF).
11. St. Augustine, *Enarrationes in Psalmos*, XC, i, 1 (LF).
12. St. Augustine, *Sermo* CCV, 1 (LF).
13. John Henry Newman, "The Cross of Christ the Meaning of the World," *Parochial and Plain Sermons*, (London: 1870–73), Vol. VIII.
14. Phil. 2:5–8.
15. St. Ignatius Loyola, "Principle and Foundation," *Spiritual Exercises of St. Ignatius* (New York and Cincinnati: Fr. Pustet, 1894).
16. *Ibid.*, "Discernment of Spirits."
17. *Ibid.*, "The Three Degrees of Humility."

Version, Vatican Polyglot Press.
8. Statement of the Third Plenary Council of Baltimore, 1884.
9. Pius XII, Encyclical, *Humani Generis*.
10. *Ibid.*
11. Statement of the Archbishops and Bishops of the United States, NCWC news release, November 18, 1951.
12. Pius XI, Encyclical, *Casti Connubi*, Official English Version, Vatican Polyglot Press, December 31, 1930.
13. Statement of the Archbishops and Bishops of the United States, NCWC news release, November 21, 1949.
14. Pius XII, Encyclical, *Summi Pontificatus*, Official English Version, Vatican Polyglot Press, October 20, 1939.
15. John Henry Newman, *Certain Difficulties Felt by Anglicans in Catholic Teaching Considered* (London: Longmans, Green and Co., 1900–01), Vol. II.
16. Leo XIII, Encyclical, *Rerum Novarum*, Official English Version, Vatican Polyglot Press, May 15, 1891.

CHAPTER VIII

1. Matt. 5:16.
2. Matt. 5:13–16.
3. Ephesians 4:15, 4:24, 5:1–2.
4. St. Augustine, *De Civitate Dei*, XIX, xix (NF).
5. St. Augustine, *De Trinitate*, XII, xiv, 22–23; xv, 25 (NF).
6. St. Augustine, *Enarrationes in Psalmos*, CXXIII, 2 (LF).
7. Pius XI, Encyclical, *Rappresentanti in terra*, December 31, 1929, Official English

CHAPTER IX

1. Ps. 115:15.
2. St. Ambrose, "On the Resurrection," in *Two Books on the Death of Satyrus* (NF2).
3. St. Bernard, "Sermon on the Death of His Brother Gerard," in Watkin Williams, *St. Bernard of Clairvaux* (London, 1867).
4. Council of Florence, 1415–45.

5. II Mach. 12:43–45, 56.

6. Council of Florence, 1415–45.

7. James Bénigne Bossuet, *An Exposition of the Doctrine of the Catholic Church,* trans. Rev. Wm. Coppinger (New York: B. Dornin, Bookseller, 1808).

8. From "Requiem Mass on the Day of Burial," *"Roman Missal.*

9. St. Cyril of Jerusalem, *Catechetical Lecture* XV (NF2).

10. I Cor. 15:12–22.

11. *So-called Second Letter of Clement of Rome* (NF).

12. St. Augustine, *Enarrationes in Psalmos,* V, 10 (LF).

13. St. Augustine, *Enchiridion, de fide, spe, et charitate* c. 112 (LF).

14. Robert Cardinal Bellarmine, *On the Ascent to God,* trans. T. G. Gent, 1616 (London, 1928).

15. Pope Benedict XII, cited in Thomas B. Chetwood, S.J., *God and Creation* (New York: Benziger Bros., 1928).

16. St. Augustine, *Sermo CCXLII,* viii, 11 (LF).

17. Apoc. 21:1–4, 6–7, 9–12, 22–27; 22:4.

Index of Sources